COACHING A CHAMPIONSHIP HIGH SCHOOL TRACK AND FIELD TEAM

DICK COLLINS

PARKER PUBLISHING CO., INC.
West Nyack, New York

©1984 by

Parker Publishing Company, Inc.
West Nyack, New York

Library of Congress Cataloging in Publication Data

Collins, Dick
   Coaching a championship high school track and field team

   Includes index.
   1. Track-athletics—Coaching. 2. School sports
—Coaching. I. Title.
GV1060.675.C6C64 1984   796.4'2'0712   83-19385
ISBN 0-13-138967-X

Dedication

To my high school coaches:

> Mr. Louis Farber
> > Former head football coach at East Providence High School—East Providence, R.I. and Pueblo High School—Tucson, Arizona

> Mr. Edward R. Martin
> > Former Superintendent of Schools—East Providence, R.I. and former head track coach—East Providence High School—East Providence, R.I.

> Mr. Stephen Sorota
> > Former head coach of football and track—Phillips Academy—Andover, Mass.

Without the dedication, inspiration and guidance of these three men, my coaching career and this book would not have been possible

Special Thanks

To Andover High School assistant coaches:
> Richard Bourdelais
> Arthur Iworsley
> Gerry Grasso
> Gien Alsup

For their assistance in the technical aspects of this book

To Andover High School student Scott Robichaud for his assistance with the illustrations

What This Book Offers You

Twenty-eight years of experience coaching track and field at the high school level provide the basis for this book which is designed specifically for high school coaches. Building and organizing a successful program, together with the motivation, teaching and training of young athletes, is what this book is about. The basic thrust is not aimed at just the development of superior athletes, but on working with and developing the ordinary youngsters who comprise the bulk of all high school track teams. It is a rare coach, indeed, at this level who does not spend 99 percent of his or her time working with athletes who fall below the superstar category; in fact, most of the young people we deal with in high school fall far below that distinction. The purpose of this book is to give you the tools and insights to deal with the realities and day-to-day problems we all face in high school track and field.

This book is not exclusively a technical manual on track and field. A multitude of technical manuals have been written by the greatest experts in the game. Coaches who read this book have a command of basic techniques in the various events and access to the best technical literature on the subject. The purpose here is to concentrate mainly on the coaching of these techniques. A separate chapter is devoted to each of the events in track and field and attention is given to first presenting each event to prospective candidates, then to the process of teaching the event, and to tried and proved training methods for high school athletes. A major feature of the book is a section in each of the technical event chapters devoted to analyzing the most common faults found among high school competitors, the main causes of those faults and the means to correct them. This is not just a book on technique, it is a book on coaching.

No matter how knowledgeable you may be as a coach in the techniques of track and field and how good a teacher you may be, it is all in vain if the athletes are not there. It is an old adage of the profession that you cannot coach what you do not have. All great coaches are masters of recruiting and motivation. Track and field programs do not become outstanding by accident; the sport does not promote itself. The opening chapter, therefore, presents methods of getting youngsters out for the team, holding them, motivating them, and promoting and publicizing the program. Particular emphasis is given to selling track and field to the coaches and athletes of other sports, especially football.

Possibly the most significant and successful motivational feature of this book is the "Goal" or "Next Immediate Objective" system, tied into a unique letter award system, that has worked wonders in motivating young athletes, particularly those with little or at least undeveloped ability. This system is guaranteed to promote both interest and progress in high school level competitors. The "Goal" system, along with the promotion of the team concept in track and field, also carefully explained, have been the key tools employed successfully over the past twenty-eight years.

It is no secret that successful coaching in all sports at all levels requires superior organization. The complexity of track and field makes this factor more important in our sport than in any other. That is why organization is given major attention in this book because the greatest of effort and the best of intentions can still result in little of productive consequence without careful planning and organization.

Utilizing assistant coaches to their maximum is essential to any winning program. It is the thesis here that the best way to accomplish this goal is to combine the boys' and girls' programs. The advantages of combining programs are outlined in detail along with the organization and planning that go into a joint program. Enthusiasm for girls' track permeates throughout this work. Girls' programs have given a tremendous boost to high school track and field and schools that are not tapping this resource and utilizing it to strengthen both teams are missing out on a tremendous organizational and motivational weapon. Although it is the general thesis of this book that girls should be coached no differently from the boys, there are, of course, certain differences and these are carefully analyzed in the discussion of each event as well as in dealing with problems of recruiting and motivation.

Organizing practices may be the most difficult task of the high school coach when you consider the multiplicity of events in track and field, the large numbers of participants, the whole variance in experience and abilities, and the frequent doubling and tripling of athletes often in unrelated events. Twenty-eight years of experience in organizing practices in both football and track and field provide the background for the practice organizations presented in this book. Ways are shown to gain maximum teaching effectiveness from the staff, maximum supervision, and maximum efficiency of the athlete's practice time.

Simultaneous boys' and girls' meets at the same site generate great enthusiasm for track and field if long delays and drawn-out meets can be avoided. A major feature of the book is a detailed structure for running combined meets both at the dual and multi-school levels that is guaranteed to increase the numbers of spectators and generate new interest in the sport.

No team can ever be successful without a firm commitment to and acceptance of standards of conduct essential to championship performance. A unique system for establishing discipline and democracy in a program is presented. You will see how to utilize peer pressure as a positive rather than a negative influence upon the behavior of young people in a way that enhances a track and field program.

Psychology plays a major role in the motivation of athletes, in their performance in the various events, and in the entire coaching process. A full chapter is devoted to analyzing the four key psychological areas with which we must cope as high school coaches: dealing with youngsters who are not getting the most out of their ability, for a variety of reasons; combating the phenomena of "their way vs. your way"; developing the proper state of mind for both practice and competition; and, most important of all, dealing with young athletes as human beings. The coach, to be successful, must be able to deal with the psychological problems with which we are all faced. This aspect of coaching is a major thrust of this book, not only in Chapter 3, but as a constant theme throughout.

This book is aimed at the realities of high school coaching. I have had my share of great athletes and championship teams, but like everyone, I have also labored through difficult years when the talent just wasn't there. I have traveled the full road, the good years and the not so good, that all of us experience at one time or another. The most difficult task of the high school coach is coping with less than ideal facilities and conditions, as well as with average and often mediocre talent. It is with these realities in mind that this book is presented.

Dick Collins

Contents

CHAPTER 1

PROMOTING A HIGH SCHOOL TRACK AND FIELD PROGRAM

Track and field coaches have the greatest product in the athletic world. No other sport offers a better combination of individuals and team, and a greater opportunity for the widest variety of athletic types and abilities. Nowhere else can you get the same degree of fellowship in a competitive situation. Nevertheless, to be successful you must get out and sell it. The coach who feels a track and field program will sell itself is in for a rude awakening in this age of multi-sport programs in the modern high school. We cannot sit back and expect hordes of youngsters to come marching to our banner. Baseball, soccer, football, basketball and hockey, with their elaborate youth programs, have the first crack at young athletes. We have to let people know what we have to offer and the beauty of it is that we have such a unique product to sell.

More than any other athletic activity track and field lends itself to mass participation. The traumatic experience of cutting from the squad, for both athlete and coach, does not have to take place in track and field. In our three-year school of roughly 1,500 students, averaging 150 girls and boys participating each year, not a single soul has ever been cut. Even if you have no assistants, you can always make a place for any youngster who really wants to participate in track and field. Further, track and field is the one sport where progress in every aspect can be easily and objectively measured. No matter how lacking in athletic skill an individual may be, improvement and achievement can always be attained and accurately measured. We do indeed have a great product to sell.

Possibly the greatest skill any coach can possess is the ability to motivate. You have to get the youngsters out, keep them out, stimulate them to achieve and make them want to come back for more each year. In this chapter we shall deal with tested methods of motivation and promoting the sport.

A. RECRUITING ATHLETES FOR TRACK AND FIELD

1. Track and field a numbers game

More than any other sport, track and field is a numbers game. There is no great secret to our past success in track; we simply outnumbered and out-motivated our opponents. Eventually, our rivals began to catch on and we cannot do this anymore. We still work very hard at getting youngsters out and motivating them, but our opponents now do the same and many schools in our league have large numbers of participants and excellent programs. It is now much more difficult to get to the top than it used to be, but our league has developed into one of the very best in the state and we are proud of that fact.

Numbers are a major key to success. A team with just one strong competitor in each event does not stand much of a chance against a team with three or four. Everybody has bad days, but the team with real depth makes up for it with somebody else picking up the slack when a top performer has an off day. When you are shy on numbers, a key individual's absence or poor performance can result in your getting swept in an event. You don't run into sweeps very often and still win track meets. Unlike other sports, you do not have a first string on the field and substitutes sitting on the bench in track and field. No matter how much depth you have in football, it is always eleven vs. eleven on the field at any given time; in basketball there are never more than five vs. five. Of course, bench strength is important in these sports, but in track and field it is not a matter of bench strength but of more first stringers. If I have thirty outstanding athletes on my team and you have ten, it is never a question of ten vs. ten with my stronger bench; it is my thirty vs. your ten. Once in a while your ten may have a super day and beat me, but not often.

For these reasons you must concentrate on getting as many good athletes out as possible and keeping them out. The goal of a high school coach should be to build as strong a dual meet team as possible. In doing so, the more good athletes you can get out for the team, the greater the percentages are in your favor of having some of them develop into the kind of competitor who can win or score in major competition and win championships. You cannot manufacture the superstars. Certainly you can improve and motivate the good ones, and can be the difference in a potentially great athlete's success or failure, but you cannot build a champion if the talent isn't there. You can, however, manufacture a strong dual meet team out of average athletes. If you concentrate on developing numbers, the gifted ones will rise to the top and the championship will come. If you neglect numbers and the average athlete to look for the superstar to work with, you may be in for a long wait.

2. Seeking out prospects

In our school, each season all sports have a common starting date. After all the teams are called out, I start beating the bushes for potential track athletes. Waiting for the other sports to be called out is important for two reasons: first, you do not want the image of trying to steal athletes from fellow coaches, and second, it is nice to see who will come out for track on their own.

I compile a potential prospects list and begin to call out these individuals soon after the initial team calls have been made. They fall into three basic categories.

(1) Students who have been identified by our physical education staff, through their testing program in the fall, as having potential talent in some phase of track and field.

(2) Students who are hard workers in the classroom and who have demonstrated dedication and a good attitude in areas other than athletics.

(3) Students who have achieved some success and have demonstrated a good attitude in a sport that runs in a different season from track and field.

In seeking out recruits, it is important to make them feel he or she has been selected because of some strength that could be an asset in track and field. Youngsters like to be singled out and made to feel special. Don't let them get the idea the team is hurting for people and you are just looking for bodies. Convey the idea that they have at least one of the attributes necessary for success in track and field and that you feel they could make a contribution to the team. I always approach these youngsters in a low key manner; high pressure salesmanship is not appropriate. Point out the value of athletics in general and track in particular, make them feel important that you have made a special effort to single them out, tell them they are the type of person you want on the team, and then send them home and let them sleep on it. Ask them to come back and see you within the next couple of days if they are interested.

Track and field is not a sport in which many youngsters have competed on an extensive basis at the youth level. There are many out there who may not realize they have potential in the sport. Often it is just the fact that someone has shown an interest in the youngster and has sought him or her out, that convinces a student to join us and give it a try. I have recruited a large number of individuals who have become outstanding track and field athletes in this way and even a greater number of fine human beings with whom it has been one of the great joys of my life to work.

Approach differently the athlete with talent in track who is well aware of that talent and just drags his feet on coming out. I call these youngsters in, tell them they are foolishly throwing away a talent that hundreds of youngsters would give their right arms to possess, and impress upon them they are running out of time and may never get another chance. I have seen a number of individuals with a poor attitude execute a 360-degree turn around and become contributing members of the team simply because I laid it right on the line with them. I make them aware that I really don't want them with their present attitude, but if they are willing to make the effort to give me a full commitment, then I will bend over backward to help them. Never beg this type, never condone a poor attitude, but never close the door completely either. Teenagers do change; never give up on a youngster.

3. Selling the football coach

There are many good athletes, and some very outstanding ones, who are members of teams that are not in season with track and field. Go after these youngsters, especially the football players. Football represents a gold mine of potential talent for track and field. Be sure to tap it.

Since I am also the head football coach and my number one assistant in football also holds the same position in track we have no problem in dealing with the football people. Many track coaches do, however, and hopefully the following approach will be helpful in attaining the football coach's cooperation. There is no question the football and track programs can work together for the mutual benefit of both.

Football coaches are all into off-season programs and must be if they have any hopes of being successful. The off-season programs are designed to develop the players in four basic areas: (1) strength, (2) speed, (3) agility and (4) flexibility. I contend track and field can do all of these things and do them better than an off-season football program because track combines these areas with a spirit of individual and team competition within the framework of a supervised and disciplined team situation.

Sit down with the football coach, share with him your weight training, flexibility and running programs and show him you can better accomplish what he is after in a formal competitive situation than he can in his off-season program. Even if you agree to include a 10-15 minute agility-quickness drill into your daily practice sessions for weightman-lineman types, you are not going to hurt your track program. In fact, a daily emphasis upon agility and quickness may well benefit your weight events people. Particularly emphasize the importance of the competitive development an athlete will gain from track and field. In a tight spot in a football game give me the shot putter who knows what it is like to be behind on the last throw of a major competition, or the sprinter who has repeatedly faced the starting gun, any time over the youngster who has never done anything in the off-season other than pump iron. Convince the football coach you can not only do a better job of improving his people physically, but you can tremendously improve them as competitive athletes as well. You can give them far more than they would ever get in a traditional off-season program.

Once you get the football people out, however, do not make the mistake of giving them special status. This goes for athletes recruited from any sport for that matter. When you get talented athletes of this type out you must insist they are full-fledged members of the track team. They are expected to make a full commitment to track and field and to contribute to the success of the team. You do not need or want individuals who are just using track and field to get ready for another sport and whose presence weakens team discipline and hinders the intensity of your practices.

If I were coaching only track and field, I would make sure that I had at least one member of the football staff as an assistant with the track team. The tie-in becomes much stronger when people on the football staff are directly involved in the track program. Equally important is having a member of the physical education department on your staff if you are not teaching in that area yourself. These people have contacts with every youngster in the school and are in the best position to spot potential talent.

4. Recruiting girls

All this is just as important with the girls as it is with the boys, and in some cases more so. Of course, there is no football program to tie in with, but there are many outstanding girl athletes in other sports whose talents you can tap. Further, there are many more girls than boys who may not be aware of their athletic potential. Our school has now as many varsity teams for girls as it does for boys, but the great explosion in girls' athletics is still a fairly recent development. Girls do not have the extensive youth programs that are available to the boys and our culture still holds them back to some degree, although that is rapidly changing. Numbers pay off for the girls just as they do for the boys, in fact, quite possibly more so as the chances are that most girls' teams against whom you will compete will not have the numbers of their male counterparts.

In recruiting girls pay careful attention to two crucial factors. First, it is necesssary to get to girl prospects earlier than the boys. Girls mature faster than boys and are frequently ready for varisty competition a year or two earlier. The fact that we are a three-year high school and our 9th-grade girls are not eligible for varsity competition hurts our girls' program considerably while it has little if any impact upon the boys' team. It is vitally important to begin building the girls' program as early as possible as many girls will be peaking athletically in their freshman and sophomore years. In gymnastics, swimming, running and jumping, it is not uncommon to see girls, as they develop physically, begin to lose efficiency of performance as they reach the last year or two of high school. This is not true of all girls, but it is true of many. For this reason it is very important that you get girls involved in track and field as early as possible.

The second major problem is getting strong, good-sized girls out for the weight events. We get plenty of girls out for this area of the sport, and some of them have done quite well, but most often they are not big girls and are not physically equipped for real stardom. The most successful girl we have had in the weights was tall but not hefty. She was also attractive, popular, and came from a family prominent in national athletics. She definitely did not have a poor self-image of herself and that is the key in this area. Girls who have the physical equipment to be outstanding in the weights, especially the shot put, often do not have a good self-image because of their size, and the thought of being a shot-putter only compounds that already negative self-image. Whereas size and strength are status symbols for boys, our culture has not reached a point where the same is true for the girls.

Dealing with this problem is a major dilemma. I have actually had girls hide from me when they heard I was looking for candidates for the weight events. Some even feel insulted when you approach them. The key to success in recruiting this type, and it is the area with which I have had the most difficulty, is attacking that self-image. The female coach can deal with this better than the male but she is not immune to the problem. Seek the assistance of female guidance and physical education people in attempting to recruit such girls. Emphasize that the type of training you are proposing will trim the figure not expand it. Nothing motivates a youngster like success and stress the fact that great achievement is possible in this area of the sport. There are fewer outstanding girls in the weight events than in any other aspect of track and field; the opportunities are tremendous.

5. Sharing the athletes

One final point in recruiting: do not insist that your athletes eat, sleep and drink track, or even that track be their primary sport. It is certainly advantageous to have that type of youngster, but if you expect every team member to be in that category, you are not going to have very big squads. We have had a number of our athletes go on to win full football scholarships at top colleges who did outstanding jobs for us in track although it was not their primary sport. We also have a great basketball tradition and have had many super basketball players make fine contributions to our track team as a secondary sport. Conversely, the athletic development and the competitive experience they gained in track and field were factors in their success in basketball. Our basketball success is the work of our outstanding basketball coach, but we take pride that we have made a contribution toward it. Certainly they have made a contribution to us. The same is true to some degree in all sports in our program. Our championship football teams have been loaded with track men and our championship track teams have been loaded with football players. In some cases track was the youngster's primary sport and in some cases it wasn't. It really makes no difference as long as the individual gives 100 percent to the track program while he is in it.

Track is a numbers game and there is no better way to build numbers on your team than by developing a spirit of sharing the athletes in your school. Specialization may be a fact of life in the colleges and pros, but it is not necessary at the high school level, and certainly not below that. Coaches who push 8- and 9-year old youngsters into one sport full time are not thinking of the athlete's welfare but of their own success. It is very difficult to predict where a youngster's talents will eventually lie at such an early age. So many of these youngsters are talked into putting all their eggs into one basket and they come up empty. Coaches who try to dominate young people 12 months out of the year are selfish. Work hard to promote a spirit of cooperation and sharing of the athletes in your school and community and everybody will benefit from it. Winning breeds winning—share the athletes and everbody can be a winner.

B. MOTIVATING TRACK AND FIELD ATHLETES

1. The goal system

Probably the greatest enthusiasm builder in our program is what we call the "Goal System." Actually, goal is not the best word to describe this system, but it has become traditional with us and we continue to use it. What we have done is set up a system of next immediate objectives for every athlete in each event. We post a huge chart in both our boys' and girls' locker rooms. All team members are listed on the chart along with their goals, or next immediate objective, for each event in which they participate. Every time a youngster achieves a goal, or immediate objective, the achievement is recorded on the chart and a new goal is set. Each goal reached results in the athlete's being awarded a point toward his or her varsity letter. If, for example, a youngster had a goal of 48' in the shot and threw 48'2" in a given meet, we would record the achievement on the chart by circling the goal just attained and by listing a new goal of 49'. When the athlete in question betters the new goal of 49', we would so record, set a new goal, etc.. Some of our athletes might make 7 or 8 goals in a particular event in the course of a season.

In every event we post minimum goals, although in extreme cases we may set an initial goal lower than the minimum or basic for an individual particularly lacking in athletic skill. You can be as flexible as you want to be in this regard. The important thing is that the goals be realistic and achievable for the athlete. Goals can only be achieved in regular meets or in practice competition that is announced in advance as a goal day. The latter is not used for regular varsity competitors, but is used as an incentive for those who may not get the chance to compete on a regular basis. It is our definite policy to be sure that every member of the team has at least one chance each week to make his or her goal or goals.

The goal system avoids the dilemma created for youngsters who have no chance in a given season to work up to the varsity level. A 35'

SAMPLE GOAL SHEET

John Brown:

Shot Put			Discus		
Goal	Perf.	Date	Goal	Perf.	Date
40'	40'5	4/15	120'	121'3	4/15
41'	41'9	4/19	123'	125'8	4/19
43'	43'1	4/26	127'		
44'					

Joseph Smith:

100			200			Long Jump		
Goal	Perf.	Date	Goal	Perf.	Date	Goal	Perf.	Date
:10.8	:10.8	4/15	:24.0	:23.8	4/15	18'	18'3	4/19
:10.7	:10.6	4/19	:23.7			19'	19'1	4/26
:10.5						19'6		

shot-putter, for example, who is up against a 48-footer for the fourth and final varsity position is going to have a difficult time seeing the light at the end of the tunnel and can easily get discouraged. Knowing that there is a letter point waiting for only a one-foot improvement gives that individual a very realistic incentive.

The enthusiasm this system has generated is fantastic. Many of our rivals have adopted it and vouch for its success. I have actually seen a young man run 5:59.7 in the mile, breaking his goal of 6:00, and be carried off on the shoulders of his teammates, some of whom were state class competitors. The above youngster never scored a point for us in varsity competition, but his elation at that experience may well have been the most satisfying moment of my coaching career. The beauty of our sport is that prograss is so easily measured and we should take pains to capitalize on it. If anything I do has merit, this goal system is it.

2. The letter system

An interesting paradox in our part of the country is that although wearing a letter sweater has long been out of style, an extremely unfortunate development in my opinion, the winning of a varsity letter is still a matter of considerable prestige. Such an award has tremendous significance to our young people and the letters are proudly displayed on bedroom walls, etc.. We use the varsity letter as a major incentive factor in our program and have developed a rather unique point system that has been a very strong motivating tool. The point system is strict and rigidly enforced.

LETTER POINT SYSTEM

(1) Each point scored in a varsity meet counts as one point toward a letter. Relay points are divided among the team members.

(2) Each goal attained in our goal system counts one point toward the letter.

(3) Every regular practice attended counts one point toward the letter.

(4) Every meet participated in or attended by a team member who is not an actual participant counts 2 points toward the letter.

(5) Major meets hosted by our team count 10 points for all participants and 10 points for squad members who serve as hurdle crew members, pit carriers, field event markers etc..

(6) Attendance at practice sessions held during spring vacation week counts 10 points toward the letter. This little refinement is designed to discourage vacationing right in the middle of our spring season.

(7) Points are deducted for unexcused absences or other violations of team rules. This will be discussed in the section on team discipline. We deduct 10 points for any unexcused absence from practice and 20 for an unexcused absence from a meet. The latter has never been a problem but the provision is there just in case.

(8) One point is granted for every season of track (indoor or spring) and cross country in which an individual has participated prior to the current season.

The number of points required for a letter is determined by totaling the number of practices and meets on our schedule for the season, taking into consideration all 2- and 10-pointers, and adding 5 to the total. In this way a youngster who participated in cross-country, indoor and spring track the preceding year and cross-country and indoor track the current year, and who never missed a practice or a meet for any reason the entire season, would be eligible for a letter even though he or she never scored a varsity point or achieved a goal.

I am not worried about arguments that we are cheapening a varsity letter by making it possible for the super-faithful youngster to qualify. Nor am I concerned about the varsity-caliber performer who doesn't qualify because of rules violations. They earn the points or they do not make the letter, it is as simple as that. We reward the traits that really matter, not just athletic skill. The important thing about any letter system is that the standards are set well in advance, everybody knows exactly what they are, and that they are rigidly and fairly enforced. This system rewards the conscientious youngster and penalizes those who do not have the kind of attitude we all look for. I am convinced the system promotes the proper attitude and has motivated individuals to stay with the team who might otherwise have become discouraged and fallen by the wayside.

3. Motivation through recognition

(1) The newspapers

Publicity is a key factor in generating enthusiasm in track and field. We do not have the bands, cheerleaders and other fanfare that go along with other sports, nor are most of our meets overflowing with spectators. An athlete getting his or her name in the local newspaper for placing in a dual meet might well be the only public recognition that youngster ever gets. Don't sit back and take what the papers give you; get out and do something about newspaper coverage. If you have a local paper that does not give track athletes a fair shake, keep on its back until it does. The squeaky wheel usually gets the grease. Haunt them with information about your athletes. Often, the papers are looking for space fillers. If necessary, write the articles yourself or have a manager or one of your bright team members do it. We live in a publicity-conscious society and young people crave recognition. Make sure they get it.

(2) Bulletin board and newsletter

An excellent motivating factor is a team bulletin board placed in a conspicuous place. In addition to pertinent information on coming meets, entry lists, etc., post point-scoring totals, newspaper write-ups, pictures of team members, stories and pictures of alumni who are still competing and anything else you feel will provide recognition and motivation. A newsletter given to team members and sent out to parents, interested supporters and alumni can be equally effective.

(3) Awards

Individual awards can be extremely motivating if handled properly. We have six memorial awards in honor of former team members and boosters. We present outstanding performer awards to both boys and girls for both indoor and spring track. We also present an outstanding attitude award for both boys and girls track. You can give as many or as few as you wish, for whatever achievements you wish. "Rookie-of-the-year," "most improved," "most dedicated," "contributed most to the team" are just a few of many possibilities. The key is to be sure that the awards are truly merited and are presented in an atmosphere of dignity. If you present the awards in a manner that conveys your belief that they are important, your athletes will treasure the recognition. We also present "Guts" awards, simple certificates of an appropriate nature which we give out to some individual whose performance in a particular meet represented a special effort and contribution. These "Guts" awards have a great deal of meaning for our athletes, and, since they are presented after every meet, have a very special impact. The key to any system of awards is presenting them in such a fashion that they serve as an incentive to bigger and better performances and team contributions.

(4) The team party or banquet

It is extremely important to finish every season with a special occasion and on a high note. Our track team holds a season-ending party at my home and it is the climax of the season. A formal banquet can be equally effective. In our particular situation we have a formal banquet for the football team which has been a tradition for almost 25 years. Since I am the football coach and many of my athletes are on both teams, the house party represents a pleasant change of pace. I happen to have a large yard, a cooperative wife, and, my one extravagance in life, a swimming pool. Our party is like an outing and the youngsters play softball, touch football, swim, etc. all afternoon. The cost is minimal as the coaches buy the soft drinks and each team member brings a favorite dish from home, and we have a fantastic smorgasbord.

At the conclusion of the day we all assemble on the front lawn for the presentation of letters and awards, the announcement of next season's captains and a few words of wisdom and good-bye from the outgoing captains and coaches. We average 150 boys and girls at this party and, if nothing else, it proves that teenagers can have a good time without drinking or smoking pot. This is just our way of ending the season; the formal banquet is just as good. The important thing is to do something. Finish the season on a high note, regardless of how well you did in competition during the season. This is what the seniors will remember and it will contribute to bringing the underclassmen back for more.

C. A TRACK BOOSTERS CLUB

A track boosters club or a parents' organization can be of tremendous value to a high school program as long as you keep a direct hand in it and do not let it become a pressure group. Try to involve as many people in this type of organization as you can. Our boosters officiate at all our meets, engage in fund-raisers for whatever projects seem to be appropriate and are generally there when we need them. Try to get alumni and interested track fans in the community involved as well as parents. We invite our boosters to our track party and utilize them in the presenting of our awards. Involving the community in your team creates enthusiasm for the sport and your program, and this enthusiasm rubs off on the athletes. I have similar organizations in both football and track and would find it difficult to operate without them.

D. HOSTING MAJOR TRACK MEETS

A great way to promote track and field in your community is to host major meets at your facility. If you do not have a good enough facility, get out and starting fighting for one. Sell the mass participation angle and emphasize that with a proper facility you can encompass the values of both interscholastic competition and intramurals all in one package within your program. Educators and school boards love the concept of mass participation and getting their money's worth. Hit hard on this approach, organize the community behind you and get a decent facility. Once you get it—make full use of it.

1. Host your own invitational meet

Even if your facility may not be of a quality to host major championships, you can still run your own invitational. Twenty-three years ago, before we had our present fine facility, we started a meet sponsored by our Boosters Club that is still a highlight of our season. We limit the field to ten teams, not for the sake of winning as we invite outstanding teams both from within and outside our league that give us all we can handle, but to provide an opportunity for a large number of youngsters to have the thrill of scoring in a major meet atmosphere. An open-style meet is fine, but in this type of competition only the very outstanding usually have much chance of placing. We want as many of our athletes as possible to walk home with a medal in this meet. Our opponents in the meet, of course, have the same opportunity.

In this meet we offer memorial trophies in each event in honor of former boosters who have passed on, as well as establishing trophies in a few events in honor of some beloved "old timers" who are still with us. This creates a lot of good will and is an inspiration to our athletes. One of our rival schools runs its own invitational in indoor track and has named each event in honor of a recent alumnus who was particularly outstanding in that event. This is an alternative approach that has a great deal of merit. It is amazing how much a "John Smith Memorial Javelin" or a "William Brown 100 Yard Dash" means to people, and how much it can do for your program.

2. Hosting major championship meets

Hosting league, district or state championship meets at your facility can be a tremendous boost to your program and will generate a great deal of enthusiasm in the community. Hosting a major meet involves a lot of work on the part of everyone—yourself, the assistant coaches, the athletic director and the team members who put out mats, lug hurdles, etc., but it is well worth the price. People will come out to watch major competition, especially if the meets are well run and sufficiently publicized. Pre-high school youngsters in the community will see good track and field and develop an interest in the sport. Holding a major championship meet at your facility becomes a showcase for your program.

Hosting a meet also gives you a competitive edge and an honest one. Your athletes compete on a facility with which they are familiar and are freed from the burden of travel and the necessity of hanging around all day waiting to compete. Coaches who are unwilling to pay the price of hosting a major meet are in no position to begrudge the edge you get by so doing. It takes time and effort on your part, you never get anything for nothing, but it will generate enthusiasm, promote your program and give your athletes a not insignificant competitive edge. I would walk the extra mile for these things any day. In 1980 Andover hosted the State Relays (boys and girls), the Andover Boosters Invitational (boys and girls), The Northern Area Championships (boys and girls), the State Class A Championships for Boys, the State Class A Championships for Girls, and the State All-Class championships (boys and girls). Hosting six major meets in one season was going overboard to say the least and was the result of some extenuating circumstances, but the point is we were willing to do it and the benefits far outweighed the price.

E. THE IMPORTANCE OF THE TEAM
CONCEPT IN TRACK AND FIELD

The team concept is often neglected in some track and field programs. Some even regard track and field as an individual and not a team sport, but I contend the team idea should be pushed to its fullest. A major value gained in participating in athletics is learning to become part of a team and to work together with others toward a common goal. Although track and field also embodies the values of individual competition, I contend it can also develop team values just as readily as any of the so-called team sports. We treat track and field as a team sport and preach this concept every day in talks to the team and by example.

Every school day practice we do our opening calisthenics or flexibility exercises as a team, both boys and girls together, with the captain out front leading. When these are completed the entire team takes a lap together, usually accompanied by chanting or cheering, and then assembles in the stands for the head coach's daily talk. At this point I cover any administrative details that need attending to, explain the objectives of the day's practice, go over the schedule for the week and finish up with some words on the importance of team, working together, winning with humility, losing gracefully, etc.. I keep it short and sweet and base the subject on whatever seems appropriate at the time. These little sessions are very important and tend to pull the team together. There are character-building aspects of athletics but never be fooled into assuming they come about automatically. You have to continually tell youngsters what you believe in and what you expect of them, taking care not to appear as though you are preaching, and then demand they meet your standards. Of course, you must sincerely believe in them and practice them yourself. If there is one thing teenagers are expert in it is spotting a phony. These little meetings take about 10 minutes each day and I am convinced they are the most important 10 minutes we spend.

In competition the successful coach is always looking for the edge, as long as it is an honest one. Anything gained by cheating or breaking the rules is not worth the price. The team concept in track and field brings about an extremely significant edge to the individual competitor. An athlete who is competing not just for himself or herself, but for the team as a whole, has a special extra incentive that often turns defeat into victory in individual competition. Observe at a major championship meet the difference in emotion between athletes whose team is in contention for the title and those who are on teams with no chance for the team title and are competing basically just for themselves. There are, of course many athletes who are very highly individually motivated, but for most, the difference just described is very pronounced. It is no coincidence that teams in contention for a team title continually come up with little better than average athletes scoring when not expected to do so, often beating superior competitors. Motivation is a key to athletic success, and the track and field coach should never neglect the importance that the team concept plays in this respect. Even if you have a poor group of athletes and have no change for a team title in a particular meet, set some sort of a team goal anyway, impress upon the youngsters that the goal is significant and then react accordingly when they achieve it. The athlete who is motivated by both the reward to himself or herself and by the reward to the team, has a distinct advantage over the athlete motivated only by personal success.

If one disagrees with the concept of track and field as a team sport, then I would suggest that person has never seen the impact of momentum upon athletes in a highly competitive meet. I have seen many dual meets turn completely around when one team scored an unexpected sweep in an event or when some one scored an upset over one of the opponent's star performers. The enthusiasm generates over the rest of the team and individuals begin to perform far above expectations. The youngsters must be thinking team, however, in order for this to happen. Further, just the fact your athletes care about the team, and consequently for each other, cheering for each other and rooting each other home, can be the difference in bringing about an outstanding performance and can be the difference between winning and losing.

CHAPTER 2

ORGANIZING A HIGH SCHOOL TRACK AND FIELD PROGRAM

A. STAFF ORGANIZATION

1. Combining boys' and girls' programs

The first step in organizing a high school track and field program is to determine the makeup and assignments of the staff. During the first few years of my coaching career I handled 17 events by myself. At the time this was no big deal and just about everybody in those days worked without assistants. Fortunately such a situation today is extremely rare. In the present era a head coach is definitely handicapped without qualified assistants and it is vitally important that these assistants be utilized in the most efficient manner possible.

I am convinced the best way to utilize coaching personnel is to combine the boys' and girls' coaching staffs. The fewer events each coach handles, the better the job that coach can do. An individual working with 40 youngsters in 8 events, for example, is not going to give the same caliber of teaching as the coach handling 40 athletes in 4 events. We have combined our staffs for three basic reasons: (1) to gain greater efficiency in the utilization of the staff, (2) to establish better coordination of the practice equipment and facilities, and (3) because I was becoming excited at the development and enthusiasm our girls were showing and wanted them to have the same coaching advantages as the boys. We have combined our program for five years now and my only regret is that we did not do it sooner. Working with the girl athletes has become one of my great joys in coaching.

2. Assigning staff responsibilities

The head coach should always assign assistant coaches the events in which they are strongest and handle the rest himself. It is a major error, in my judgment, to put assistant coaches in charge of areas in which they are not comfortable and have little expertise. It is absolutely vital to get the most out of your assistant coaches if you want to have a successful program. If the head coach has a particular expertise in a certain area, it is difficult to turn those events over to an assistant. Certainly, the ideal is to have all coaches, including the head coach, working in their strongest events. If a sacrifice has to be made in this regard, however, it is better that the head coach take over a particular area than to knowingly create a weakness in his program by turning over to an assistant events that he or she cannot handle.

There is no one way that a staff should be organized. It depends on the number of coaches available and the event expertise of each individual. We currently have five coaches on our staff. This was realized by combining a former organization of a boys' head coach with two assistants and a girls' head coach with one. Our staff is organized in this manner:

(1) *Head Coach:* 100, 220, 440, 440 relay, mile relay—Boys and Girls.
(2) *First Assistant:* Boys' high and low hurdles, Girls' hurdles, high jump Boys and Girls, and pole vault.
(3) Assistant A: Boys' and Girls' long jump, triple jump.
(4) Assistant B: Shot, discus and javelin—Boys and Girls
(5) Assistant C: 880, mile and two mile—Boys and Girls

This is not presented as the ideal organization; it is the best for our situation and the coaching personnel we now have. Whatever you do, do not place an assistant in charge of a group of events unless that individual has sufficient expertise to teach those events properly. In many cases it will be necessary to take someone with little knowledge of track and field, but one who cares about young people, is dedicated to coaching and eager to learn, and train that person yourself.

Assistant coaches definitely should have full responsibility for the events they are assigned to handle. You cannot expect to get true dedication from an assistant if that individual is used primarily as a baby sitter. All assistants must work in close cooperation with the head coach and there must be definite consultation on major decisions, but do not expect dedication and loyalty from an assistant if you are unwilling to delegate authority to him or her. To get maximum efficiency from the coaching staff, each member must be given responsibility for a certain group of events. A coach who tries to handle too many events, as we did in the old days, often spends most of his time making sure nobody is getting killed. Specialization in track and field coaching has taken over. This is why we have combined our boys' and girls' programs and our coaching staff, limiting as much as possible the number of events each coach handles. There is absolutely no reason in the world why boys and girls competing in the same events in track and field cannot learn and train together.

B. ORGANIZING A PLACEMENT AND TESTING PROGRAM

The first two weeks of the season all first-year people, as well as any veterans who have not yet really established themselves in a particular event, should be put through a testing process. During this period everyone in this category, what we call the general track group, are given flexibility work, technique running, conditioning running and weight training and are put through the testing process. The testing does not have to be elaborate, and each coach is given a free hand to conduct the testing any way he wishes. In some cases, such as the shot, discus and high jump, we simply allow the beginners to try the event with a bare minimum of prior explanation. Since our outdoor pits are not ready when the season opens, the long jump-triple jump coach utilizes standing long jumps, standing triple jumps, jump reach tests and an evaluation of the sprint tests in his area. In the javelin we use a softball throw while in the pole vault we actually put the prospects on the pole, with the coach assisting by grabbing the pole and raising it to the vertical, as described in the pole vaulting chapter. Hurdlers are tested by running over a low hurdle, while running potential is assessed in 50, 440, 880 and 1-1/2 mile runs. Subject to adjustments due to weather and other circumstances, our basic testing schedule is as follows:

Day 1— Orientation and general conditioning
Day 2— High jump—shot put
Day 3— Long jump—hurdles

Day 4— Triple jump—discus
Day 5— Pole vault—softball throw (javelin)
Day 6— 50 yd. dash—1-1/2 mile cross country run
Day 7— 440 yard run—High jump, shot, discus for those who missed earlier tests.
Day 8— 880 yard run—Hurdles, long-triple jump, javelin for those who missed earlier tests.
Day 9— All re-tested in 50 and 1-1/2mile, pole vault for those who missed earlier test.
Day 10— General catch-up day for missed tests.

At the end of the testing period we hold a staff meeting and run through all the individuals who have undergone the testing process. There are always a few exceptions whom we place very quickly due to extremely obvious talents, but most of our youngsters are not assessed until this meeting. As I read off each name, the various coaches indicate if they feel a particular individual belongs in their area. If there is no dispute, the youngster is assigned to the coach who put in the bid for him. If more than one coach indicates an interest in someone, we then pull out every bit of information we have on that individual, including initial records on weight training status and personal perference expressed on the registration sheet, discuss the matter thoroughly and then make a decision. We do the same thing if no coach indicates an interest in the youngster. In some cases it is necessary to divide a youngster's time with two coaches until we can establish a more accurate evaluation.

Great care should be taken in testing, evaluating and placing individuals in event areas. Don't ever let this become a haphazard affair. It is easy to make mistakes and coaches must be open-minded and flexible regarding event placement as the season progresses. It is a tragedy if promising athletes never reach their potential because we, as coaches, fail to recognize where that potential lies.

C. PRACTICE ORGANIZATION

In organizing practice sessions there are basically two types with which we all deal. The first are the practices on school days when everyone is on the field at once. The second type involves non-school day practices when the athletes can be spread out over a staggered schedule and more individualized and specialized coaching can be accomplished. Both of these types of practice sessions will be discussed in this section.

Each coach should be responsible for organizing the day's workout in his event areas. As said in the previous chapter, you cannot expect maximum production out of assistants if you do not give them authority and responsibility. It is necessary, however, for the head coach to be informed of what the assistant plans to do in the next practice sufficiently in advance so that he can offer suggestions or recommendations and that necessary coordination can be established. The head coach must coordinate the use of the weight training equipment, scheduling its use so that it will not result in overloading of the area and equipment at any particular time. Obviously, the less equipment you have, the greater a problem exists in this area. Second, the head coach must coordinate the practices of those individuals who compete in events that involve more than one coach. On high school track teams it is very common for sprinters to compete in jumping events, for a hurdler to high jump or throw the javelin, etc.. It is necessary to do some real thinking and planning to be sure your athletes are getting the most out of each practice to meet their individual needs and that each assistant coach is being utilized to his maximum.

One very important rule, that should always be followed, is that every athlete should have a primary event. If a youngster is doubling or tripling, then primary and secondary events must be designated. If, for example, an athlete is designated as a long jumper for his or her primary event and runs as a sprinter as a secondary event, then that individual should be trained as a long jumper and sent to the sprint coach for the running part of the workout, with the responsibility for all training decisions in the hands of the long jump coach. That athlete is trained and treated as a long jumper and is used in the sprints for gravy points. If you train an athlete 50-50, you will get somewhere around 50-50 efficiency of performance in each event. Once in a while a superstar may disprove this theory, but the occasions will be rare. I would suggest also that even with the superstar, if you brought him or her to the ultimate test of ability, say at the national level of competition, and trained that individual in two different areas, that athlete would be beaten by an individual of equal ability and dedication who has concentrated full training in that one event.

If you have large numbers, it is a good idea to split up the athletes in each event into beginners and advanced groups, and, in some cases, an intermediate group might be included. We use this concept particularly during non-school day practices, but will also employ it at times in certain events and situations during regular school day sessions. The more you can narrow the number of events in which an assistant can specialize, the more appropriate this type of organization becomes. Level of technique development rather than performance level should be the main criterion for such group placement. There is no reason whatsoever why boys and girls cannot work together in the same groups.

It is also important to avoid sending groups off to work by themselves. It is virtually impossible to avoid this completely, but unsupervised work should be kept at the barest minimum. In the more dangerous events, of course, it should never be allowed. The running events do not present the same problem as the field events, but if in the latter a system of rotating groups working on technique, running and weight training is employed, it is possible to keep unsupervised technique work down to a minimum. Also, judicious placement of field event areas can allow coaches to keep a direct eye on, and control of, more than one activity. In our situation this is particularly true for our coach who handles the pole vault, high jump and hurdles, as well as for our long jump and triple jump coach. Unfortunately we do not have the same luxury in dealing with the three throwing events.

1. Organizing practice on school days

On school days the entire team assembles at the same time. Everyone jogs a lap together, does calisthenics and flexibility exercises together as a team, follows this up with another group lap and then assembles in the stands for a short team meeting. After the team meeting, ten minutes is allowed for what we call build-ups. Build-ups involve 3 laps of 6 × 220's, alternating 55 yards jogging, 55 yards striding (gradually increasing on each stride segment from 50 percent to 90 percent), 55 yards of jogging and 55 yards of walking. This entire process takes roughly 30 minutes and is standard for all practice sessions.

Basically we run 2-1/2-hour practice sessions on school days. We use a standard two-hour session, following the initial warm-up period, divided into 24 five-minute segments. This is a practice followed by many football teams and works equally well in track and field. After discussion with each assistant on what he plans for the coming day, I put together three organization charts. The first is broken down by events, the second by coaching assignment and the third involves organizing the practice of those individuals who compete in more than one event and who cross over to more than one coach. (See Charts A, B and C.)

2. Sample practice schedule—combination events coaching crossover

The most difficult area of practice organization lies in the coordination of the schedules of athletes doubling or tripling in events. If

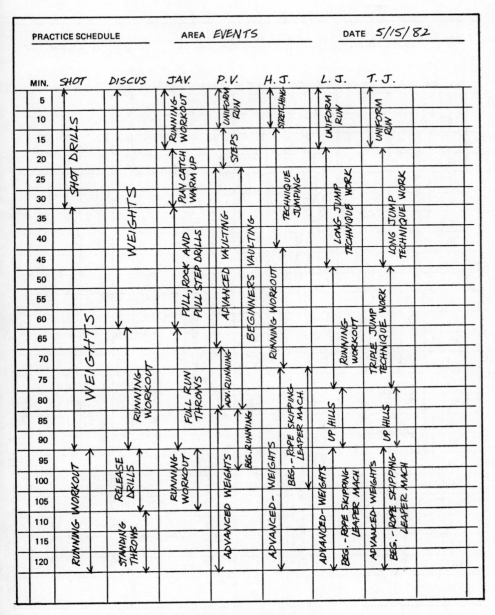

CHART A   Practice Schedule—Events

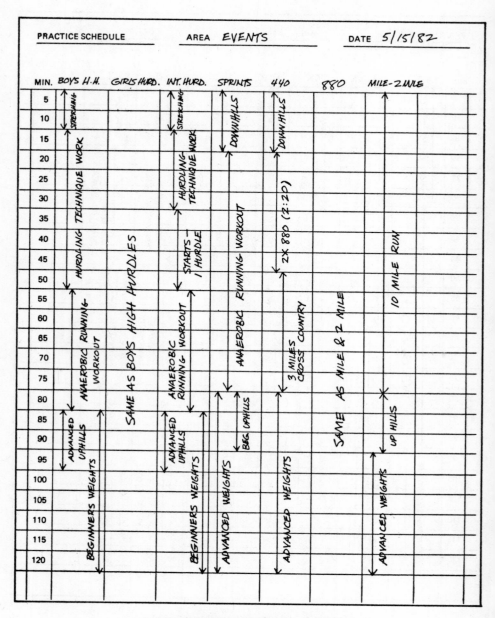

CHART B   Practice Schedule—Events

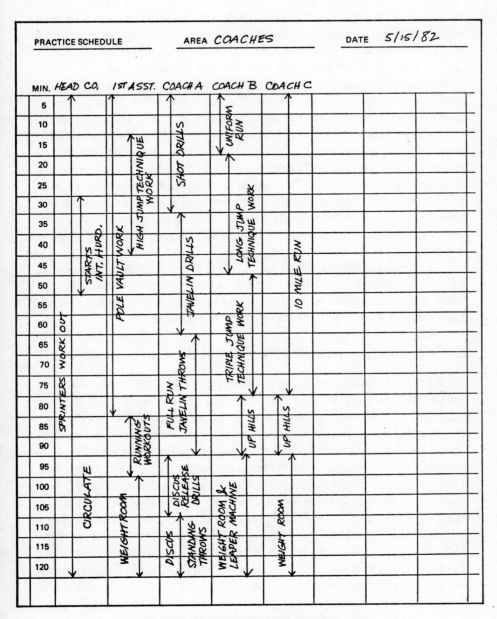

CHART C   Practice Schedule—Coaches

the combination lies totally within a particular coach's responsibility, it becomes his task to work out the day's schedule within the prescribed workouts set for the events involved on that day and the coach's own schedule. If the combination of events involves coaching crossover, then it becomes the responsibility of the head coach. It is important when dealing with this problem always to keep in mind the primary and secondary event concept. There are some days when it is most feasible to keep the athlete with his or her primary event. In most cases when there is a crossover, the most reasonable objective is to schedule the youngster in the secondary event when the coach is working on technique and devote the remainder of the practice, and certainly the bulk of the session, to the primary event. No matter how it is handled, there has to be some sacrificing made in both areas. The goal is to keep such sacrificing at a bare minimum in the primary event and recognize that considerable give will have to take place in the secondary event. Placing a superstar in this position would appear to be a questionable tactic if progress in the primary event is the major consideration.

In the sample schedule (Chart D), the top athlete involved in each particular combination is listed with the combination of events, the primary event listed first. Any other athlete involved in the same combination would follow the same day's practice schedule.

3. Organizing practice on non-school days

Practice sessions on non-school days involve a great deal more work on the part of the coaching staff, but they are the days when the best coaching is done because more time is available, the workouts for each event can be staggered, beginners and advanced competitors can be worked separately and the coach can concentrate on each event free from distractions. The organization is simpler also as the practice is spread out. Our policy is to do the technique work first in each event, then, if a field event, the running portion of the workout and finally the weights on alternate days. It is impossible to create an ideal situation for all combination athletes. The schedule is set up to best meet the needs of as many individuals as possible. If the combination involves a running event and a field event it is best to work in the technique portion of the field event first and then the running event workout. This doesn't always permit the athlete in question to get the running workout in at the same time as the specialists in that event, but our running event coaches are still in a position to supervise the workout.

Charts E and F show the basic non-school day schedules we have utilized for years. In a given year it may be adjusted slightly to better meet the needs of our combination event athletes.

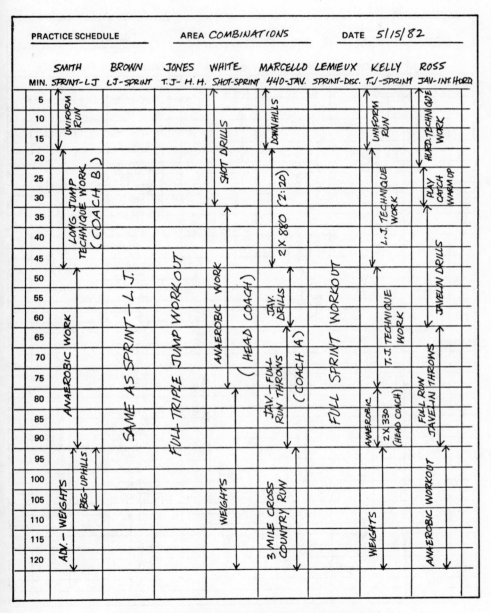

CHART D   Practice Schedule—Combination Events

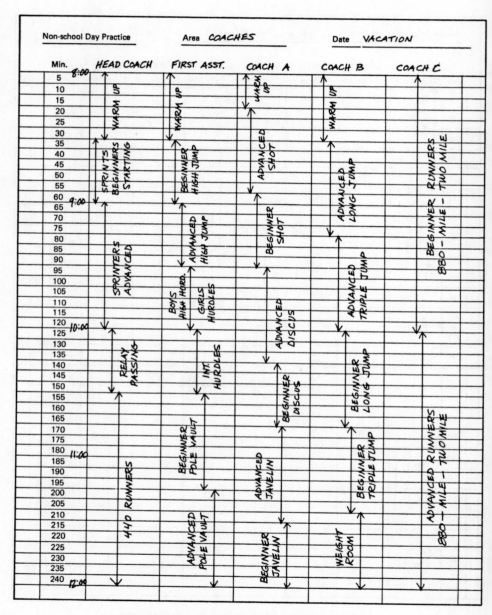

CHART E   Non-School Day Practice—Events

Non-School Day Practice		Area EVENTS		Date VACATION
Event	Report Warm up	With Coach	Running	Weights
AVANCED SHOT	8:00 – 8:15	8:15 – 9:00	9:00 – 9:30	9:30 →
ADVANCED LONG JUMP	8:00 – 8:30	8:30 – 9:15	9:15 – 9:45	9:45 →
BEGINNER SPRINTS	8:00 – 8:30	8:30 – 9:00	9:00 – 10:00	10:00 →
BEGINNER 880 – MILE – 2MILE	8:00 – 8:30	8:30 – 10:00	—	10:00 →
BEGINNER HIGH JUMP	8:00 – 8:30	8:30 – 9:00	9:00 – 9:30	9:30 →
ADVANCED SPRINTERS	8:30 – 9:00	9:00 – 10:30	—	10:30 →
ADVANCED HIGH JUMP	8:30 – 9:00	9:00 – 9:30	9:30 – 10:00	10:00 →
BEGINNER SHOT	8:45 – 9:00	9:00 – 9:30	9:30 – 10:00	10:00 →
ADVANCED TRIPLE-JUMP	8:45 – 9:15	9:15 – 10:00	10:00 – 10:30	10:30 →
BOYS HIGH HURD. GIRLS HURD.	9:00 – 9:30	9:30 – 10:00	10:00 – 11:00	11:00 →
ADVANCED DISCUS	9:15 – 9:30	9:30 – 10:15	10:15 – 10:45	10:45 →
INT. HURD.	9:30 – 10:00	10:00 – 10:30	10:30 – 11:30	11:30 →
BEGINNER LONG JUMP	9:30 – 10:00	10:00 – 10:45	10:45 – 11:15	11:15 →
ADVANCED 880 – MILE – 2MILE	10:00 – 10:30	10:30 – 12:00	—	12:00 →
440	10:00 – 10:30	10:30 – 12:00	—	12:00 →
BEGINNER DISCUS	10:00 – 10:15	10:15 – 10:45	10:45 – 11:15	11:15 →
BEGINNER POLE VAULT	10:00 – 10:30	10:30 – 11:15	11:15 – 11:45	11:45 →
BEGINNER TRIPLE JUMP	10:15 – 10:45	10:45 – 11:30	11:30 – 12:00	12:00 →
ADVANCED POLE VAULT	10:30 – 11:00	11:15 – 12:00	11:00 – 11:15 12:00 – 12:15	12:15 →
ADVANCED JAVELIN	10:30 – 10:45	10:45 – 11:30	11:30 – 12:00	12:00 →
BEGINNER JAVELIN	10:45 – 11:00	11:30 – 12:00	11:00 – 11:30	12:00 →

CHART F Non-School Day Practice—Coaches

D. ORGANIZING A WARM-UP PROGRAM

One of the greatest problems in coaching track and field at the high school level is convincing young athletes of the importance of proper warm-up. It is vitally important that warm-up procedures in practice are properly supervised and that everyone is impressed with the necessity of following the same procedures in competition. Some coaches warm-up their entire squad together before every competition, but this is impractical. In competition everyone is on a different time schedule and premature warming-up makes no sense and can even be extremely counter-productive. No matter how much the coach talks about it, some youngsters are not going to be convinced and they will "save their energy" instead of warming-up properly prior to competition. As a coach you can never take warming-up for granted. There is no way an athlete can compete at maximum efficiency without proper warm-up.

We require that every team member jog a lap, go through our full program of calisthenics and flexibility exercises and then jog another lap before every practice and competition. Athletes in the throwing events then start their throwing warm-ups and all runners and jumpers do three laps of 6 × 220 build-ups (described in the section on practice organization). This is the bare minimum of warm-up. Warming-up is strictly an individual process. Each individual must determine for himself or herself, with the guidance of the coach, just how much warm-up is necessary to be at maximum efficiency when competition begins. Through trial and error, each individual must determine how much additional running, if any, how many preliminary jumps or run throughs, and how many throws put that particular athlete at the point of maximum efficiency. As a general rule we suggest 30 minutes of warm-up and 15 minutes of rest, keeping loose before competing, but this is strictly general and many athletes need more than this. Some might possibly even perform best with less, although such an eventuality is rare.

There is no need to go into a calisthenics and flexibility program in a book of this nature since all coaches are familiar with these programs. It is pertinent to emphasize the importance of flexibility both to gain maximum efficiency of performance and avoid injuries. A few years back we brought in a woman from our town who is a yoga expert and she put in our entire flexibility program, which we have been using ever since in both football and track. Most communities have experts of this nature and the coach who does not tap this valuable resource is missing a good thing. We do not get into the meditation aspects of yoga, just the flexibility work, body alignment and breathing. These people know what they are talking about and you can really benefit from drawing on their experience.

Like everything else, flexibility is an individual matter. Some athletes are going to need more work than others in this area, although no one can be too flexible, and certain events will need extra work. The important thing is to get a good program in operation, supervise it carefully, and make sure your athletes follow the same procedures in competition that they do in practice.

E. ORGANIZING A WEIGHT TRAINING PROGRAM

Weight training is absolutely essential for maximum performance in all events in track and field, and, in my opinion, in all sports for that matter. No one is strong enough and everyone benefits from increasing strength. Obviously it is more important in some events than others, but everyone can benefit from a proper strength program. The old myth that existed when I was a competitor that weight training makes an athlete muscle-bound is simply not true unless the youngster is into the Mr. Universe concept. Properly run, weight programs will help everybody.

Essential to a good weight training program is a proper facility, good and sufficient equipment and proper full-time supervision. None of us at the high school level have truly ideal conditions and many of us, this author included, have to make do with far from what is desired. Regardless of the circumstances under which you must work, you must constantly work, and fight if necessary, to get the best facility, equipment and supervision possible.

There is no aspect of athletics that can get you into more trouble as a result of improper supervision than weight training. First and foremost there is the safety factor. Improper lifting techniques and fooling around can lead to serious injury. The weight room must be orderly and there must be a seriousness of purpose among everyone involved. Since it is unlikely that a high school will have a separate weight room for every sport, and certainly not for track and field, it is essential that all coaches in the school work together and cooperate on the weight room's use. Ideally, if the school provides a full-time weight room supervisor, who works closely with the coaches, your track program will benefit tremendously.

1. Areas of concern in weight training

There is no area of athletics in which youngsters are reluctant to listen to the coach like weight training. How am I going to look at the beach may be the single most significant motivator to youngsters in the weight room. There are several key problems with which you must deal if you wish to get maximum results out of your strength program.

(1) Many youngsters avoid the exercises that they do not do well because it makes them look bad or feel inferior. There is a great deal of ego involved in weight training.
(2) Some youngsters are a bit timid in the weight room and frequently never get to the equipment sufficiently because the pushy ones are hogging it.
(3) Many are the beach athlete type who are only interested in doing the exercises that will make them look good.
(4) You will always have a few clowns—their activities must be curbed or a serious accident can result.

If anyone thinks the above categories are not a problem, then I suggest that he or she has never been in an unsupervised weight room.

2. Essentials of all weight training programs

(1) Observe all safety precautions religiously.
(2) Be sure all equipment is in proper condition.
(3) Provide proper supervision.
(4) Be sure all weight training is progressive. Regardless of what system is being used, there must be progression if strength is to be gained. This involves periodically increasing weight or repetitions or both as a particular program gets easy.
(5) Weight training should be at least on an every-other-day basis. You must give muscle fiber sufficient time to repair itself. Some weight trainers work on different areas of the body on consecutive days, and I see nothing wrong with this although we do not practice it, but never work on the same muscle groups on consecutive days.
(6) Be sure to work on all areas of the body. If the athlete concentrates on certain favored muscle groups the gap between strong and weak areas of the body increases. In time of stress the weak muscles always bear the brunt and this is when injuries take place. The beach athlete types are most often the victims of this. All athletes will pay the price of neglecting to work on certain areas of the body.

3. Basic weight training programs

(1) Weight machine

Like most schools we have a weight machine and feel it is the safest and most convenient system of weight training. We have benches, squat racks and free weight equipment also but not in adequate quantity to meet the needs of a squad as large as ours. As a result we put all our girls and inexperienced athletes on the weight machine. The standard weight machine workout includes:

Station 1— Bench press
Station 2— Military press
Station 3— Front trunk twists (1 set of 25)
Station 4— Forearm curls and upright rowing
Station 5— Kneeling alternating pull downs
Station 6— Dips (1 set of 25)
Station 7— Leg press
Station 8— Inclined sit-ups (1 set of 50)
Station 9— Leg lifts (off machine) (1 set of 50)
Station 10— Leg extensions and leg curls (small machine)

(2) Free weights

The standard free weight workout includes:

1. Bench press
2. Behind the neck military press
3. Inclined press
4. Squats
5. Heel raises
6. Clean and jerk
7. Forearm curls
8. Upright rowing
9. Inclined sit-ups (1 set of 50)
10. Leg lifts (1 set of 50)
11. Leg extensions (Small machine)
12. Leg curls (Small machine)

(3) Nautilus equipment

Although we do not have Nautilus equipment in our school, I am extremely high on its potential for track and field because of its safety and convenience factors as well as its providing an excellent program working on all parts of the body to develop endurance and flexibility as well as strength. We are fortunate to have a commercial Nautilus facility less than half a mile from the school manned by personnel extremely interested in track and field. Obviously we can only encourage youngsters to join this program, but a number of them do and we have seen definite positive results particularly with runners and jumpers. If we have individuals enrolled in the Nautilus we either let them go when weight training comes into their schedule or we work out a schedule with them individually that allows them to work it in. I keep in touch with the people that run the facility to be sure my athletes are working out properly. This has not been a problem as the type of youngster who puts out money for such a program is the type of dedicated athlete you do not have to worry about.

(4) Flexibility in the choice of equipment utilized

My major concern is that all team members be involved in some form of strength training. I prefer the free weights for the weight events and the weight machine for girls and inexperienced boys, but I am not about to get into an argument with a youngster over which equipment to use. Some of our athletes, for instance, may be into a program with the Nautilus or weight machine for basketball and if they wish to continue, I am not about to force them into free weights. There is a great deal of psychology involved in weight training. If a youngster prefers a particular type of equipment and is dedicated to using it, don't force him into something else. There is always more than one way to skin a cat.

4. Types of weight training workouts

(1) Regular workouts

Our regular or standard type of workout involves 3 sets of 10 repetitions each on all exercises except sit-ups, leg lifts, and the weight machine dips and trunk twists. We use a weight that results in some straining around the 7th repetition and considerable strain but not the loss of good form on the 10th. In theory, if an athlete can make the 11th repetition in good form, there is not enough weight and 5–10 pounds should be added. If the youngster cannot make the 10 repetitions in good form, then you are using too much weight. It is always safer and wiser to start off with too little weight and work up than it is to attempt it the other way around.

(2) Heavy workouts

Bulking-up is a term well known in weight training and is the result of working with heavier weights and less repetitions. There is a great deal of merit in utilizing this type of workout for weight men in the off-season and in the first weekly lifting session during competition. If you follow the principle of working up to full intensity as outlined in the description of regular workouts, it obviously necessitates utilizing less repetitions when increasing the weight load for any exercise. Our standard heavy workout entails 3 sets of 5 repetitions. This means the final repetition will be accomplished with considerable strain but still in good form, and an additional repetition will not be possible. 3 sets of 5 is not sacred, however, and any combination of sets and repetitions can be used as you see fit. A 5-set sequence of 6-5-4-3-2 repetitions, for example, also has merit. The important principle is the less repetitions used, the greater the weight load, always working up to full capacity or intensity. Care should be taken when working on exercises that can effect the leg joints. For this reason it is a good policy to keep leg curls and leg extensions on a regular rather than a heavy workout basis.

(3) Explosive workouts

In an explosive workout we utilize 60 percent of the weight used for a particular exercise in a regular workout, still using 3 sets of 10 repetitions. These repetitions, however, are done as rapidly and explosively as possible while maintaining good form. This, of course, applies only to those exercises where weight is involved and would not include sit-ups, leg lifts, dips, trunk twists, etc., if those exercises are included in an individual's program.

F. ORGANIZING COMBINED MEETS

1. Dual meets

Combining our boys' and girls' meets (on a separate scoring basis) has added great enthusiasm to our program and has increased spectators at meets. The key to successful combined meets is continuous action. We are bound by a league order and state regulations that prohibit competition in more than 3 events, only 2 of which may be running or field, and only one running event over 440 yards. The organization we utilize works well and may give some insight into organizing your own situation.

(1) Field events

Group A— Girls' high jump
Girls' discus
Boys' long jump
Boys' javelin
Boys' pole vault

Group B— Girls' long jump (immediately follows boys' long jump)
Girls' javelin (immediately follows boys's javelin)
Boys' high jump (immediately follows girls' high jump)
Boys' shot (immediately follows boys' javelin)
Boys' triple jump (immediately follows boys' long jump)

Group C— Girls' shot (immediately follows girls' javelin)
Boys' discus (immediately follows boys' shot)
If we had only one pit we would place the triple jump in Group C.

(2) Running events

Girls' Two Mile—Beginning of Group A Field Events
Girls' JV 100
Boys' JV 100
Girls' JV 440
Boys' JV 440
Girls' JV 880
Boys' JV 880
Girls' JV 220
Boys' JV 220

Girls' 100 Meter Hurdles—At completion of Girls' Long Jump
Girls' JV 100 Meter Hurdles

Boys' 120 High Hurdles—At completion of Boys' High Jump
Boys' JV 120 High Hurdles

Rest of running events follow immediately after Boys' JV High Hurdles:
All varsity:

Girls' 100
Boys' 100
Girls' one mile
Boys' one mile
Girls' 4 × 110 Relay
Boys' 4 × 110 Relay
Girls' 440
Boys' 440
Boys' 330 low hurdles (Intermediates)-Varsity & J.V.
Girls' 880
Boys' 880
Girls' 220
Boys' 220
Boys' two mile
Girls' 4 × 440 Relay
Boys' 4 × 440 Relay

At the beginning of the meet, at the same time Group A field events are starting we run the girls' Two Mile. This is followed immediately by all JV races except the hurdles. The girls' hurdles are run immediately following the completion of the girls' long jump which always completes before the boys' high jump. At the completion of the boys' high jump we run the boys' hurdles and then follow immediately with all other running events in the prescribed league order. Girls' running events are contested in the same order as the boys' from this point on and always precede them. JV hurdle races follow varsity races. Field events in Group C and the pole vault may well be in competition while the varsity running events are going on.

2. Invitational combined meets

Our ten-team Booster's Invitational is one of the highlights of our season. It is a combined scoring boys' and girls' meet which generates a great deal of enthusiasm and exciting competition. In organizing any meet of this nature the key is having enough officials and support personnel. We draw on boosters, alumni and parents for officiating assignments. To run an invitational meet properly you need:

(1) A meet referee
(2) A chief official for each field event
(3) Two clerks of course
(4) A head judge and timer
(5) Judges for each place and timers for each place with 3 clocks on first place for record purposes
(6) A minimum of 3, 5 if possible, for the press box
    1. A chief scorer with an assistant if possible
    2. A custodian of awards with an assistant if possible
    3. An announcer
(7) A minimum of 30 support people taken from the JV's or non-competing varsity
    1. A 10–20-member hurdle crew, one or two individuals to each flight
    2. 2 people to handle the bar in the high jump
    3. 3-person crews for all other field events to serve as markers, tape holders, pit rakers, spotters and pole catchers in the pole vault etc.
(8) A 3-person crew at the finish line to handle the finish yarn and lap cards

A multi-school meet that is well planned in advance and has enough officials and support people will go off smoothly and interestingly for spectators.

The order of events we utilize provides for constant action and can be completed in a reasonable time. In analyzing the following order it should be recognized that we are bound by Massachusetts regulations that allow only one running event, one field event and one relay for each athlete in major competition. We are also limited to one running event over 440 yards.

COMBINED INVITATIONAL BOYS' AND GIRLS' MEET

Order of Events

Field Events: 11:00 A.M.

Girls' High Jump
Girls' Discus
Boys' Long Jump
Boys' Pole Vault
Boys' Shot Put
Boys' Javelin
Girls' Long Jump (follows boys' long jump)
Girls' Shot Put (follows boys' shot put)
Girls' Javelin (follows boys' javelin)
Boys' High Jump (follows girls' high jump)
Boys' Triple Jump (follows boys' long jump)
Boys' Discus (follows girls' discus)

Running Events: Group A: 11:15 A.M.

11:15—Girls 100 M Hurdle Trials
11:30—Girls' Two Mile
11:45—Girls' 100 M Hurdle Semi Finals
12:00—Girls' Mile
12:15—Girls' 100 M Hurdle Final
          Group B: 12:45
12:45—Boys' 120 High Hurdle Trials
 1:00—Girls' 220 Trials
          Boys' 220 Trials
 1:15—Girls' 100 Trials
          Boys' 100 Trials
 1:30—Boys' 120 High Hurdle Semi Finals
 1:40—Girls' 220 Semi Finals
          Boys' 220 Semi Finals
 1:50—Girls' 100 Semi Finals
          Boys' 100 Semi Finals

2:00—Boys' One Mile
2:15—Girls' 440
     Boys' 440
2:30—Girls' 880
     Boys' 880
2:45—Boys' 120 High Hurdle Final
2:55—Girls' 220 Final
     Boys' 220 Final
3:05—Girls' 100 Final
     Boys' 100 Final
3:15—Boys' 330 low (Intermediate) Hurdles
3:30—Boys' Two Mile Run
3:45—Girls' 4 × 110 Relay
     Boys' 4 × 110 Relay
4:00—Girls' 4 × 440 Relay
     Boys' 4 × 440 Relay
4:15—Presentation of Awards

G. TEAM RULES AND REGULATIONS

The single most important area of coaching is the establishment and fair enforcement of team rules and regulations. These are the basis of control and discipline of the team. No matter how much you know and how concerned you may be, if you do not have control of the team and there is no discipline, there will be no coaching success. Make only those rules that are necessary for success, keep them simple, be sure they are well understood in advance and enforce them rigidly and fairly.

1. The Winner's Committee

A Winner's Committee is established each season for the boys' team and a separate one for the girls' team. This committee is made up of the team captains, two seniors elected by the seniors, two juniors elected by the juniors, two upper classmen appointed by the captains (the team is never informed who was elected and who was appointed by the captains), and one sophomore, elected by the sophomores, who sits in on cases involving sophomores only. This committee sits and determines punishments within our rules and regulations in all cases involving violations of those regulations.

The Winner's Committee is one of the best things we do and it serves two important functions. First, it involves the athletes in the team, creating a feeling that this is really their team and that they have something to say on how it is run. Second, it serves as a real deterrent to the breaking of team rules. Peer pressure is possibly the single most motivating factor among teenagers. It is so often a negative factor in their lives, why can't we as coaches make it a positive one. Our athletes simply do not want to go before the Winner's Committee and, consequently, we get few violations of team rules. That, after all, is the bottom line. The purpose of any system of this nature is not to punish violators but to promote behavior that will lead to team success.

2. Rules and regulations

(1) All team members must be at all practices and meets unless excused in advance by a member of the coaching staff. Penalty for unexcused absence: deduction of 10 points toward a letter (20 if it is a meet), suspension from the next meet, appearance before the Winner's Committee for possible further action.

(2) Smoking, drinking and taking drugs are prohibited. Penalty for violation: deduction of 20 points toward the letter, suspension from the next meet, appearance before the Winner's Committee.

(3) Lack of respect for fellow team members, coaches, officials and opponents will not be tolerated. Unsportsmanlike conduct, deliberate profanity, tardiness at practice and loafing or failing to give maximum effort will also not be tolerated: Penalty: at coach's discretion. Chronic violations will result in appearance before the Winner's Committee.

(4) Show respect for all school facilities and equipment: The theft or destruction of school equipment requires complete restitution and a hearing before the Athletic Director.

(5) Finish what you start. Quitting is not allowed. If you do not wish to make a full-season commitment to track and field do not come out for the team. (We can do much about this but we put all kinds of pressure on our athletes on this subject. I make a commitment to them, I expect them to make the same commitment to me. I make sure they all understand this when they come out. In 28 years of coaching, quitting has been less than 1 percent.)

When an athlete appears before the Winner's Committee that individual is presented with his or her violation of the rules, is allowed to state his or her case, is questioned by the committee members, and then is dismissed while the committee makes its decision. In dealing with the case the committee has three alternatives:

(1) They can increase the penalty established by the rules: This could be suspension from additional meets, further letter point deduc-

tions, work details carrying equipment, etc., additional running, push-ups, etc. (only for those athletes whose training program would not be hindered by such action), or even removal from the squad.

(2) They can leave the penalty as it stands in the rules.

(3) They can recommend that the penalty as it stands in the rules be reduced or eliminated altogether because of extremely extenuating circumstances.

It is important in dealing with a Winner's Committee that the coach accept its decisions. The whole concept breaks down if the athletes begin to think you want the committee merely as a rubber stamp. If I feel the committee has been too excessive or too lenient I will meet with it and discuss the situation and possibly lead to a modififcation of their decision. It is extremely rare that I ever do this and if I fail to get the committee to see my point of view I will stick with their decision. As I said before, the purpose of the Winner's Committee is to create a spirit of team and an atmosphere that lends itself to living by the rules. It has been an extremely effective tool toward that end.

DEALING WITH FOUR MAJOR PYSCHOLOGICAL ASPECTS OF HIGH SCHOOL TRACK AND FIELD

One often hears at football coaching clinics the expression, "X's and O's don't win football games—people do." Sometimes we forget the wisdom of this statement, yet it is probably the most important truism found in coaching all sports, and particularly track and field. As coaches, we are not dealing with robots into whom we program techniques, we are dealing with human beings who think and feel. Four key areas are analyzed in this chapter as far as the psychology of coaching track and field at the high school level is concerned. This is not to imply these are the only areas of concern of this nature, but they are the ones that represent the greatest challenge to the high school coach.

A. DEALING WITH ATHLETES WHO DO NOT GET THE MOST OUT OF THEIR ABILITIES

There are three types of young athletes who do not achieve up to their potential. (1) Those who do not make a sufficient effort, (2) Those who lack confidence in themselves, and (3) Those who try too hard.

1. Those who do not make sufficient effort

Basically youngsters who do not make an adequate effort fall in three categories. (1) Those who are out for the team for the wrong reasons, (2) Those who are being subjected to negative peer pressures, and (3) The lazy and spoiled.

There are some youngsters who are out for the team because of parental pressure or because their friends are out and they want to be part of the gang. In dealing with this type, a heart-to-heart talk is necessary. Deep down they really don't want to be there and are not interested in track and field success. It is necessary to get this type of individual to face up to his or her real motive for being out for the team and you have a selling job to do on the values of the sport and the benefits of success. The key in getting the most out of this youngster is to remotivate, to persuade the individual that success is worthwhile. The very fact that you sit down privately with this youngster and show you care may be the key to establishing proper motivation.

The youngster who is being pressured in a negative way against the sport may be the type who is in most serious danger. If the peer pressure is coming from friends who are pushing for another constructive activity that is one thing, but if it is coming from the element promoting drinking, drugs and non-involvement, as is most likely the case in this day and age, then the problem is very serious. The only way you are going to get maximum effort and performance out of this type of individual is to get him or her away from the negative influence. Don't attempt this by yourself; call in the parents, guidance counselors and any other interested staff members and work together seeking a solution. There is a great deal more at stake in this type of case than just track and field success. Utilize the solid members of your team as well in an attempt to get this youngster socializing with peers who possess decent values. *Combining the boys' and girls' teams is a great asset in this regard*.

If it is just a matter of a youngster's being lazy or spoiled, it is the easiest of the three categories to deal with. You first have to convince the individual involved that his or her talent is not enough by itself. This really isn't difficult to do if the youngster has pride and really wants to do well, once he or she starts to get left behind by harder working team members. If any of the other factors discussed in this section are also involved, then obviously you have a much more complicated problem. If it is just being lazy, however, sit the youngster down and get him or her to face up to it, but do it in a way that shows you care about that particular individual and are not putting him or her down. Let the youngster know he or she is going to be pushed and pushed hard because you believe he or she can take it and has the goods to be a success. Lazy people, deep down, want to be pushed so oblige them, but do it in a positive way.

2. Those who lack confidence in themselves

Confidence is nothing more than believing you can achieve whatever goal you are seeking. There are two keys to dealing with this type of individual: set realistic goals and build up the youngster's self image.

In setting goals for a young athlete, be sure he or she accepts them. This point is vitally important. It is what the youngster is seeking to accomplish that matters, not what you say he or she should achieve. The "Goal" or "Next Immediate Objective" system described previously in this book is the key to dealing with this problem. Set the goal as close to what the youngster has already achieved as possible. If he has :10.9 in the 100, set the goal at :10.8. If she has put the shot 28'9", set the goal at 29'. Sell the athlete the idea that achieving this goal is all you want from him or her. Seeking to win or score in a meet, or even beating some team member may be the worst possible objective for the youngster with a real confidence problem. Have that individual compete against something he or she can control and is obviously within reach. An extremely realistic time, height or distance is far less frightening than an opponent over whom one has no control. Once the youngster starts to achieve some success in reaching "goals" and confidence begins to build, then you can start on opponents and greater challenges.

People who lack confidence usually do not have a good self-image. Work on this by showing you have faith in the youngster. Frequently, all a person who lacks confidence needs is someone to show some faith and to give support. This is easy to do; just sit down privately with the individual and tell him or her so. Think twice about criticizing such an individual unless it is done constructively and privately. Give the youngster who lacks confidence as much support as you can and do not put him or her under undue pressure. Support from the coach and getting the youngster to walk before he or she runs are the two keys in dealing with lack of confidence.

3. Those that try too hard

These may well be the most difficult to deal with. Track and field is not one of the so-called glamor sports. It tends to attract a great number of solid, well-motivated youngsters who really want to do well. They have an intense desire to succeed, in fact so much so, they become their own worst enemies. These individuals are the ones we all love and feel sorry for because in spite of, or because of, their intensity they just can't seem to produce when it counts. The insensitive may even call these individuals "chokers," but this is a term that should never be used because it is a put-down to an athlete whose only fault is trying too hard.

The three key factors that contribute to this condition are (1) an inability to relax properly, (2) a lack of real understanding of the techniques of the event and (3) the failure to put the whole competitive process in its proper perspective.

Relaxation is the number one fundamental in track and field. If an indivdual has such intensity that he or she cannot relax properly, maximum potential is never going to be reached. The fact that you keep telling a youngster he or she is trying too hard and not relaxing does not mean that individual is accepting what you are saying. Giving everything one has is a natural instinct. It is much like the farmers during the Depression days struggling to accept the concept of the AAA that they should not work harder and produce more, but rather, take land out of production and produce less. Be sure you have really convinced your athletes on the necessity of relaxation.

One sees this problem more readily in the running events. In this area trying too hard results in straining all the wrong or antagonistic muscles and running into the proverbial stone wall. You have to keep drilling youngsters on running completely relaxed, concentrating on relaxing the jaw and fingers and separating relaxation drills from the regular workout if necessary, as explained in the chapter on running. Time them in short runs, both relaxed and straining, to prove your point. You must convince the athlete he or she can run faster relaxed and then show that individual how to do it. It is human nature to strain at the bit at the end of a race, and you must be sure you have really convinced the youngster of the folly of it.

In field events trying too hard inevitably results in putting the effort in too early. This may be the result of an inability to relax and time the explosion at the proper instant, but it also may be that the youngster just does not understand the importance of sequence in all field events. This is why such emphasis is placed upon this point in describing the initial presentation and teaching of each event in the following chapters. The athlete who tries too hard is never going to conquer the problem unless he or she fully understands what is supposed to be happening.

In all throwing events there are in general terms four basic stages— momentum, leading with the hip, delivery and follow-through. Many intense youngsters start the throw while still in the momentum stage and never get to a proper throwing position. Others may get to a decent throwing position, but then bring the arm into play immediately, eliminating the lift and hip rotation in the shot as an example, and com-

pletely losing the action of the legs. Others begin the reversing action
long before the delivery is completed. In fact, how often do we see
youngsters bring everything—hip, implement and rear leg—into play all
at once, rather than in proper sequence. You may spend hours trying to
alter technique when the real culprit is simply that the youngster is trying
too hard. Quite possibly the most important coaching tactic in the
throwing events is utilizing the expression—"Don't try to kill it—take
your time."

One sees this same factor present in the pole vaulter who gets anxious and pulls too soon, or in the high jumper who begins rotating over
the bar before completing the take-off action. How often do we see long
jumpers straining at the bit during the run up, making the same mistake as
the runner tying up in knots at the end of a race. Some jumpers are already tying up and straining at the bit before they even start the approach.
When it comes time for the explosion, they have nothing left. The culprit
in a youngster's trying too hard may well be the coach who has failed to
convince him or her of the necessity of relaxation, the importance of sequence and the correct instant for effort or explosion.

Finally, the youngster who tries too hard may simply be unable to
put the whole business in proper perspective. Without minimizing the importance of winning, it is still not a matter of life or death. The great athletes who demonstrate poise under pressure fully understand this. They
do not have a great fear of losing even though they may hate to do so.
There is a difference and it is a prime role of the coach to make athletes
aware of the distinction. The youngster who is afraid to lose gets uptight
worrying about it and inevitably tries too hard. One way to deal with this
is to get the youngster's mind off the competition as much as possible.
Encourage this type to take in a movie or some other form of wholesome
recreation the night before competition. Don't have him or her hanging
around the track any longer than necessary the day of the meet. Get him
or her off in a corner away from the excitement prior to warming-up.
Even let the individual read a book or something while waiting. Above
all, make this type aware that it is only an athletic contest and all one
expects is a good, sincere effort.

B. SELLING "YOUR WAY VS. THEIR WAY"

A second major psychological problem with which you must deal,
particularly in handling beginners, is the fact that often they are more successful doing something their own way rather than the way you are teaching. This is most true in the throwing events, but the problem exists in

every area of track and field. You must recognize and deal with this phenomenon, or the best-laid plans of teaching technique may never get off the ground. Never take it for granted an athlete accepts what you say as "Gospel," just because you say it. Just because you are absolutely certain you are right does not mean the youngster is convinced, no matter how much he or she might appear to agree with you outwardly. Young people are notoriously poor listeners (so are most older people for that matter); they learn more from what they experience than from what they hear. You have to make a concerted effort to convince them your way is best, and be absolutely sure you have convinced them.

The problem is that most youngsters will be able to throw farther, jump higher and run faster at the outset if they do it naturally rather than in some strange manner, no matter how technically sound it may be. Throwing, jumping and running are natural activities that they have been doing in one form or another all their lives. Even though they may be doing it in a technically unsound way, they do it aggressively and without thinking. (One has to be aggressive to be successful in any event in track and field.) As soon as you tell them to alter what has become a natural movement for them, they are going to start thinking about it and thinking takes away aggressiveness. Consequently, your way involves thinking and unnatural movements while their way does not; therefore their way will be more aggressive and get better results.

Before doing anything else, explain this to all beginners. A youngster must understand the importance of aggressiveness and also be convinced that *real* success will come only when that aggressivenes is combined with proper technique. They must be able to understand that everybody in track and field, especially in the field events, is going to have to go backward for a while before moving forward. One cannot improve technique without thinking about what one is doing and this is going to reduce aggressiveness and consequently results. Once proper technique becomes natural and the athlete does not have to think about it extensively, then the aggressiveness and results will come.

Once this has been explained, the next step is to be sure the athlete is completely aware of what constitutes good performance in any particular event. If you have some good returning veterans, this will become obvious to the beginner, but there are times when this will not be the case. At any rate, you must prevent a beginner from developing too great a sense of self-satisfaction with initial performance. You must make the youngster aware of what can be achieved and that only with proper technique can real success be accomplished.

The athlete who is really difficult to deal with in this respect is the one who has so much talent naturally that he or she can come out and score points in dual meets right from the beginning. Getting athletes of this caliber to take that backward step is a real problem. Their way scores points and gets their names in the newspaper, your way does not. Ideally, athletes shouldn't be put into competition until they have passed this stage, but this is not very realistic and may even cost you meets if you do so.

All coaches have had athletes with outstanding talent who never seem to reach their potential. A major possibility to consider in analyzing such a case is what is being discussed here. We have all seen athletes who look fairly good technique-wise in practice who always seem to revert back to their old ways in competition. The reason this may be happening is that the youngster is still not sold. He or she may be reverting for one of two basic reasons. (1) He or she knows you are correct but the success of the moment is more important than long-range success. (2) Deep down he still may not be convinced your way is better, no matter how much he may appear to be accepting what you say.

To win this battle you must prove to the youngster the correctness of your methods. Bring in every book, film and teaching aid you can lay your hands on and convince the youngster it is not his way vs. your way, but his way vs. the right way. Bring in former athletes you have coached who went through the backward step before achieving success and let them talk to your beginners. Don't ever take it for granted an athlete is sold on your expertise. Sell yourself and your methods, prove you are right. Remember, we live today in an era of instant gratification and instant success—never overlook this. The youngster with the greatest potential is the one who can most likely fall victim to the "Their Way vs. Your Way" phenomenon.

C. DEVELOPING A PROPER STATE OF MIND
FOR PRACTICE AND FOR COMPETITION

A third psychological problem faced by all track and field coaches, particularly in dealing with the skilled events, is the need to establish a very different frame of mind for practice as opposed to the state of mind desired for competition. An athlete who is thinking extensively about technique, especially in the skill areas, will not have the aggressiveness and explosiveness necessary for maximum performance. The objective in practice is to increase one's physical capacities, correct one's faults and improve technique. The objective in competition is top performance. The former requires a great deal of concentration on the correction of faults and technique, the latter requires supreme confidence and aggressiveness. You cannot have it both ways; there is no way an athlete can function in both states of mind at the same time.

1. The proper state of mind for practice

The worst thing a jumper or thrower can do is drag out the tape measure every time he or she practices, or put markers in the jumping pit or throwing area at specified distances. Whenever measurement takes place, the athlete is going to judge what he or she is doing by the distance achieved and not by improvement in technique. It is very easy for athletes to lose confidence in the techniques being taught if they judge each effort by the distance achieved. Once youngsters begin to lose confidence in the techniques you are teaching, it is likely they will revert back to their old ways in competition as explained in the previous section.

Athletes should never expect to perform as well in practice as in competition. Make sure they understand this and the three basic reasons why this is true.

(1) You cannot perform at your best unless properly rested. An individual is seldom properly rested before a practice session and certainly not during one. We always rest the day before major competition and taper off two days prior. Be sure that every youngster understands this so that he or she will not be constantly judging performance in practice.

(2) One's mind must be on being aggressive and there must be complete confidence in one's technique to perform at maximum efficiency. This is the state of mind desired for competition, but not for practice. In practice one must concentrate upon improving technique and, consequently, aggressiveness must be sacrificed.

(3) To perform at one's best, the adrenaline must be flowing and this comes only in true competitive situations. Convince the athletes there is no way maximum can be achieved in practice because the adrenaline will just not be there.

If you constantly put the clock on runners or put the bar at maximum height for high jumpers and pole vaulters, the same problem will be encountered, although with the former it may not be a matter of technique as much as confidence. Regardless, whenever performance is being measured in practice sessions with the clock or tape, be sure the youngster is properly rested and psychologically ready for the effort. If not, you may well be convincing the athlete of the lack of merit of your methods. Athletes judge more by what they experience than by what you tell them. Don't give them unsuccessful experiences to judge if you can help it.

It is not only imperative that an athlete not think of maximum performance in practice sessions, it is also vital that he or she not think of too many things at once. The fact you are an expert on technique does not mean the youngster has to be. It is not what you know that counts it is what the athletes working under you are able to do. Don't fill their heads with too much technical information. A major purpose of this book is to put this in its proper perspective. Give them what they need to know, but no more. If an athlete does certain things correctly, let that individual alone. This point is emphasized in the chapters on running events, but it is valid in all areas.

In step-by-step drilling it is usually not a problem, but in working on a full event do not ask the youngster to think of more than one thing at a time, and concentrate on that aspect. If the athlete is thinking about too much and you try to watch several things at once, neither is going to do the other much good. Even though the athlete must perform a complexity of techniques, it is virtually impossible to concentrate on more than one thing at a time. It is just as difficult for you to analyze more than one thing at a time. Help the athletes, do not confuse them. If there is a cardinal sin in track and field, it may well be overcoaching.

2. The proper state of mind for competition

Both the athlete and the coach must approach *competition* in a different state of mind from that of *practice*. When competition begins you are not going to correct faults or alter techniques. If you try, you are simply going to get the athlete thinking too much and destroy his aggressiveness. A young athlete must recognize that whatever form he or she has developed up to that point is the best any individual is going to get for that particular day, and full concentration must be upon getting the most aggressive performance that individual is able to attain. You must think in the same terms. If you haven't taught it in practice, you are not going to teach it in a meet.

Running events present a little different situation, but in the field events, certainly, the best thing you can do in the overwhelming majority of cases is to stay away from the athlete during competition. That does not mean you should not be in a position to observe the event. You cannot criticize later a performance that you did not see, and, obviously, you want the athlete to be aware you are there rooting for him. If a few words of encouragement during a competition appear to help a particular individual, then by all means be there to give it. A small suggestion here or there may help an athlete at times, but be careful not to get carried away, particularly if the athlete in question tends to be a thinker and worrier. Analyze each situation carefully and if you are convinced a brief comment or suggestion will help, then make it, but if not, stay away. Remember, most athletes associate the coach with thinking about technique in an intensive way. If you perform in the same manner in competition as in practice, there is a good chance it will promote the practice rather than the competitive state of mind in the athlete.

The psychological objective of the athlete in competition is vitally important. Nobody wants an athlete who does not have an intense desire to win, but if that is the youngster's only goal you can be in for serious trouble. The main goal of a competitor in track and field should be his or her best possible performance. You must never let an athlete get uptight over what an opponent might do. Impress upon each and every individual that he or she can do no more than one's best. If this is not good enough to win, so be it. You must walk a very thin line in this respect. A youngster's natural desire to win must be cultivated and you must exploit an individual's competitive instincts. On the other hand, if beating an opponent is an unrealistic goal, be sure the youngster is not thinking in those terms or a mediocre performance is likely to occur that could cost the team precious second or third place points and possibly a meet. If beating an opponent is the goal, be sure the athlete has both the physical ability and the confidence to achieve the performance necessary to win. If winning is the sole motivator, a 4:50 miler going up against a 4:20 man or a :10.6 sprinter facing a :9.9 is in big trouble. Young people are not stupid, deep down they know what they cannot do. If they feel they are expected to accomplish an unobtainable objective they are very likely to press and fall apart.

You must work hard to develop an attitude in the athletes that working up to one's potential and doing one's best are the major objectives. If a youngster begins to consistently perform up to his or her potential, the wins will come and so will the confidence. This is the most important trait you can instill in your charges. A properly prepared athlete is always confident he or she can perform at maximum effectiveness. Never put an athlete under undue pressure or let him put himself under such a burden. Preach that losing is no disgrace but not giving one's best shot is. Victories will come when the confidence is there. I have never yet seen a winner who worries about winning.

D. DEALING WITH ATHLETES AS HUMAN BEINGS

The fourth and final psychological area deals with relating to young athletes as human beings. From the psychological perspective, the major goal of the coach is to help young people develop confidence and a sense of self-worth. The youngster who possesses these qualities will not only perform better as an athlete, but will be better equipped to meet the challenges of life, and, after all, isn't that what our job is all about?

1. Sincerity

The first prerequisite for the coach in dealing with young people is to be sincere. Youngsters can spot a phony ten miles away. A coach must genuinely care about the athletes as individuals and must be himself. If you try to put on an act with young people, or if you try to imitate some highly successful coach, no matter how good your intentions might be, they will see through it and you begin to lose your credibility. Your athletes must believe in you, not just as a coach, but as a person as well. If they do not have faith in you, you are going nowhere, and being absolutely sincere and honest is the essential ingredient for gaining this faith.

2. The importance of praise

Praise is an essential ingredient in dealing with young people. They are at an age when they crave and need recognition, especially from you—the coach. Let them know when they do well and do so with a genuine enthusiasm that convinces them that their success is important to you. Let them know you are behind them in everything they do. Make it a point to go around individually to every competitor on the team in every meet and shake the youngster's hand and wish him or her well, letting him know you are behind him. When the event is over shake that individual's hand again, regardless of performance. This is very important; don't just congratulate the winners. If particular individuals didn't do well, don't be a phony; they know when they do poorly. The key is to show them you are still with them, still have confidence in them and that whatever problem exists will be resolved together. Coaches win or lose youngsters by the way they handle poor performances.

3. Effective ways to praise a young athlete

As important as a pat on the back immediately after an event may be, often it is not enough. It is a good tactic to single out an individual privately within a day or two of an outstanding performance and let him or her know how pleased you are. This is also a good tactic to use on the struggling youngsters who may not have done so well in the last meet. Let them know how much you appreciate how hard they are working and how much you appreciate their loyalty and contribution to the team. This little step might save a discouraged youngster who could later develop into stardom. Don't wait for problems to meet privately with young people. Just a little praise at the right time may well prevent problems from developing.

A very effective way to praise a young athlete is to send for him during the school day. A home room or study period can be an appropriate time for this tactic. When students are sent for in school, they often think something is wrong, especially when the coach sends for them in such cases. When they find out you sent for them to offer praise or a pat on the back, the positive reaction is tremendous. Remember, you can always find a reason to pat a young person on the back.

The quick word of praise, without stopping to talk, can also be very effective. Walk through the locker room before or after practice and, without stopping, just say to the youngster something to the effect, "I am really pleased with how well you are doing—keep it up." Singling out a youngster during calisthenics in the same manner can also have a great impact. You catch the individual by surprise, he or she looks up and sees it was the coach who said it, and is on Cloud 9 for the rest of the day.

Possibly the most effective method is to drop the youngster a note. You can send it through the school mail, make a comment on a test paper if you happen to have the youngster in class, or mail the note home. This not only has a great impact upon the athlete, but, inevitably it will be shown to the parents and with one little gesture you have made yourself two very valuable allies. I have athletes who have saved such notes for over 25 years. It is amazing how much something like this means to them. Each fall, at the end of the football season, I send a personal note to every member of the varsity squad timed to arrive the day before the Thanksgiving game. We went 22 years in a row before losing on Thanksgiving Day. When the string was finally broken it was discovered that a foul-up in mail delivery resulted in most of the players receiving their note the day after the game. This may not have had an effect upon the outcome of the game, but I have some strong feelings on the subject.

4. Effective use of criticism when it is called for

The fact that praise is used extensively as a psychological motivator does not mean criticism, when it is appropriate, is not also effective and necessary. It is vitally important, however, not to criticize or "lace out" a youngster right after that individual has done poorly in competition. This is when encouragement is essential. If criticism is necessary, do it in practice or even better in the privacy of your office. Even more important, don't "lace out" a youngster just for doing poorly. The cause may have been trying too hard and that definitely deserves a positive approach. Criticism should come for carelessness, lack of effort, failing to follow instructions or breaking team rules.

As said previously, sincerity is the first prerequisite of coaching. If you are unhappy, let them know it. Be yourself. If you have a temper, don't hide it. There are times when you have to control it, but there are also times when it can be cultivated. If you "blow up" when something is serious, they will know when you mean business. Conversely, if you want to motivate youngsters with praise, it is essential to make sure they know it is sincere. If they know you will not tolerate undesirable behavior, your praise has a much greater credibility and impact.

My old Marine drill sergeant, who always seemed to take particular pleasure getting on my back—or at least I always felt that way—came up to me privately just before boot camp ended and told me I would make a fine Marine. He probably did the same thing to just about everyone else in the outfit, but, at the time, I would have charged through 20 stone walls for him. Praise from the constant back-slapper is not nearly as effective as praise coming from someone who does not hesitate to express displeasure when it is appropriate. A little Marine Corps psychology ought to be a prerequisite for all coaches.

5. Following up criticism

We all lose our temper at times and this can be constructive, but if it happens never leave it at that. When you really lay into an individual make it a point to sit down privately with that youngster within 48 hours. Have a heart-to-heart talk and make certain he or she understands you only "blow up" at people you care about. Tell that individual what he or she did wrong, why it angered you and why it was wrong. If it turns out as a result of this little talk that the anger was not justified, don't be afraid to apologize. Nothing enhances the athlete's judgment of fairness more than the knowledge that the tough coach is not too big to apologize. It is also vital to assure the individual in question, no matter how much he or she might be in the wrong, that the matter is over and done with and there is no grudge. If punishment is necessary, give it out, and if an apology is in order, do so. Never let such a situation become negative. A very unpleasant incident can often be turned to your advantage and a hostile youngster converted into a strong ally simply by taking the time to follow up a burst of anger.

6. Double teaming

Another very effective tactic for dealing with undesirable behavior or performance we like to call "Double teaming". Sometimes it is worked out in advance and other times it is spontaneous. When one coach blows up and becomes the heavy, another assumes the role of the "good guy." Extreme care has to be taken in such a situation that the coaches involved do not undermine each other. The approach should work something like this. When one coach lays out the criticism, another takes the youngster aside when things have calmed down a bit and the angered coach is not present and says, "You know, he was right getting mad at you for that, you were not giving your best. He thinks a great deal of you and that is why he gets upset when you do not live up to your potential. I know you can do it and so do you. Let's show your coach his faith in you is justified—he wouldn't have blown up at you if he really didn't care about you."

Under no circumstances should double teaming ever be used unless the head coach and the assistant involved have discussed its use thoroughly and have complete confidence in each other's ability to use it in the right circumstances and only in a way that does not undermine either of the coaches involved. Never even consider its use with an assistant whose loyalty might not be quite 100 percent. You must have supreme confidence in an assistant to utilize this tactic, but, if used properly, it is a most effective motivational tool.

7. Dealing with personal problems

The coach's role involves a great deal more than working with youngsters in their track and field events. Often their problems have nothing to do with track and field at all. Many come from broken homes and all are subjected to some negative peer pressures. It is not the purpose of this book to get into this area as volumes have been written on this subject, but I would be remiss if I neglected to mention this vital role of all athletic coaches.

Don't try to become an amateur psychologist and never stick your nose into something that is none of your business and that you possibly do not fully understand. You can, however, work closely with parents, guidance people and staff trained in this area to help, in whatever way you can, the young people placed under your charge. At least, you can always be a good listener and show that you care. It may well be that all a particular youngster needs is a friend. You cannot solve all their life problems, the way you may be able to solve those problems that are directly connected with track and field, but you can provide understanding and that may be the one most important thing that youngsters need.

CHAPTER 4

COACHING THE SPRINTS AND THE RELAYS

Sprinters are a unique breed. They are often high-strung individuals with great pride in their ability to run fast, and are usually very intense competitors. Sprinters are born not made. You are never going to make a class sprinter out of an individual who cannot run fast naturally, but you can do a great deal to improve an athlete in the sprints, which can be the difference between success and mediocrity.

A. SPRINTING TECHNIQUE

1. Relaxation

A noted authority once said the four basic fundamentals of sprinting are relaxation, relaxation, relaxation and relaxation. As a gimmick for emphasis, I always make this statement in first meeting with sprint candidates. We once had a state champion sprinter who everybody thought was a loafer. People constantly wondered how great he would be if he only put some effort into it. The truth of the matter is that he put tremendous effort into it, but in the proper way. This young man had the talent to run relaxed. Like all the great ones, he made sprinting look easy.

Many muscles of the body have no bearing on making an athlete run faster. These are sometimes called the antagonistic muscles. An old coach of mine used to say, "Run from the hips down." This makes a great deal of sense. Compulsory reading for all our sprinters is an article written some years ago by the top college sprint coach in the nation at that time. This coach does a tremendous job of driving home the importance of relaxation by stating he doesn't want people giving 110 percent for their university. His point, of course, is not that he doesn't want people who try hard, but that he doesn't want them straining and pressing in a futile attempt to run faster.

The two key areas to stress in seeking relaxation are the hands and the jaw. If the hands are relaxed, the arms and shoulders will tend to relax with them. Tell beginners to wiggle the fingers a bit to help them relax. Similarly, relaxing the jaw tends to relax the entire upper body. There is an old axiom that it takes 37 muscles to frown and 2 to smile. I have never counted them so I am not sure this is true, but it gets the point across to the youngsters.

2. Stride length

When all is said and done there are only two factors that can make an individual run faster: (1) how fast he or she picks them up and lays them down, and (2) how much ground each stride covers. The problem is that obtaining the maximum in either area is counter-productive to the other. The fastest way to pick them up and lay them down is by running in place. Obviously, you are not going anywhere that way. Likewise, maximum stride length results in the slowest frequency of picking them up and laying them down.

The great challenge for all sprint coaches is to determine the ideal stride for each runner that will give him the most efficient combination of the two factors. Although it often may be the case, don't automatically assume that increasing a youngster's stride length is going to make him run faster. This must be done on an individual basis for every runner. No two people are exactly the same; it is a matter of trial and error and experimentation. In many cases it is obvious that a youngster's stride is either too short or too long, but with others it may not be so obvious. I am not suggesting that you should fool around with everyone's stride length. On the other hand, it is an important factor and deserves careful consideration.

3. Leg Action

The two key factors a coach should look for, where the action of the legs is concerned, are: (1) high knee action, and (2) full extension of the driving leg. Generally speaking, the shorter the race the less back kick you should see. A good sprinter lifts the knees and reaches out with the lower leg. If a youngster is not getting full extension and consequently maximum power out of the driving leg, it is either the result of not obtaining good knee lift or trying to pick them up and lay them down too rapidly. Increasing stride length is the key to the latter fault.

4. Arm action

The most important factors in arm action are: (1) keeping the arm relaxed, as previously mentioned, and (2) making sure the arm action is forward and back, or in the direction of the run, rather than from side to side. The latter error is much more common among girls than boys, particularly among those with some degree of bust development. The most important coaching point here is to emphasize keeping the elbows in close to the body. Always emphasize keeping the elbows close, the arms bent at about 50 percent, the fingers loose and the hands never going back beyond the hips or forward above the shoulders.

The faster a sprinter can move his arms, the faster he can propel his legs. This is a truism in running, provided two important factors are present. First, the speed with which the arms are used must not be at the expense of proper arm action technique. Second, the action of the arms must be synchronized with the action of the legs—right arm with left leg and left arm with right leg. A short, rapid pumping action of the arms is not going to make anybody run faster.

5. Body angle

A common fault among many high school sprinters is running with too pronounced a forward lean. Most great sprinters run with the body at a very slight forward angle. If the center of gravity is too far forward it has the same effect as handicapping a race horse with extra weight in the saddle. Conversely, a sprinter can be too erect also. The advantage of a very slight body lean over a perfectly erect trunk, with the center of gravity directly over the legs, may not be worth arguing about. If an erect trunk position results in arching the back, however, it is an entirely different matter. A sprinter must definitely avoid a backward lean or arching the back.

6. Foot placement

Once a sprinter is in full stride, the ball of the foot must strike the ground first. The drive comes off the toes but a sprinter must never run on the toes. If the heel does not make contact with the ground, the runner is going to tie up in knots. On the other hand, you do not want a sprinter running on the heels either. Most sprinters will naturally place the foot in a correct manner. Initially, I never say anything about this factor as there is no point in getting a youngster thinking about something he or she does naturally. Foot placement is important, however, and if an athlete is doing this incorrectly, you must work with that sprinter on an individual basis.

B. SPRINT DRILLS

1. Arm action

All the sprinters face the coach standing perfectly still and simply execute the arm action properly. The coach also executes the arm action and the athletes see it done properly as they do it themselves. If you cannot demonstrate this well yourself, place the team member with the best arm action out in front of the group. I like to start off many practices doing this drill for a minute or two.

2. Arm action speed

Essentially, this drill is the same as the first with the athletes starting off with a slow arm action and then, upon the command of the coach, pumping the arm as fast as they can for 6 or 7 seconds. The important thing here is for the coach to check carefully to be sure proper arm technique is not lost in an effort to make them go faster. We do this drill three times and along with the first drill described, like to begin many practice sessions in this manner.

3. High knee action

This is an exaggerated drill in that we have the sprinters run 30 yards, over-exaggerating the high knee lift and reaching out with the legs. We repeat this five times starting off very slowly and gradually working up to about half-speed. Youngsters have a tendency to lean back and arch the back when doing this and care must be taken to see this does not happen. Since most youngsters do not lift their knees high enough in sprinting, the object of this drill is to increase the knee action through exaggeration.

4. Leg extension

The Pop Up drill is good for developing leg extension. The athlete jogs along and roughly every five yards bounds straight up in the air, first off one leg and then off the other. The important thing to stress is that the athlete gets full extension of the driving leg on each pop up. We do this drill across the width of the football field seeking five pop ups off each leg on every run through.

5. Power drill

The best drill for developing leg power is uphill running. The steeper the hill, the better, and we emphasize high knee action and driving up the hill. Running up stadium stairs is equally effective. We have a convenient steep hill and prefer to use it rather than the stadium because it is a little safer.

6. Weight jacket drills

Once or twice a week we like to work our sprinters for about 15 minutes with the weight jacket. We take 10 runs across the width of the football field, alternating running with high knees with the pop up drill (#4). In other words, they will run 50 yards five times emphasizing high knee action, and run 50 yards five times doing the pop up drill.

7. Leg speed

The concept of leg speed drilling is to run relaxed and in good form with the legs moving at a faster rate than they would in normal running. There are three basic ways this can be accomplished: (1) Using a treadmill, (2) Attaching a harness to the runner and utilizing a vehicle to tow him, (3) Downhill running.

We do not have the equipment for numbers one and two, and, frankly, I would be a little hesitant to tow youngsters even if we did. We use downhill running and I am absolutely sold on its effectiveness if you do this at least twice a week over an extended period of time. The angle of decline should be slight, roughly 5–10 degrees. It is very important that the athletes retain good running technique. Have them jog into it, working up to full-out running for 30–40 yards and then easing off. We do 10 repetitions each time we do this drill. Again make sure the hill is not too steep. If the grade is too extreme you will lose good running technique and are risking injury to the youngster.

8. Relaxation running

This is a drill popularized in this area by former Olympic champion and Boston University coach Dave Hemery, which he calls "Whistlers." The sprinters start off in the middle of the curve slowly and gradually pick up speed until they are running all out as they come off the curve into the straightaway. They must concentrate on good running technique and complete relaxation. Each athlete carries the run as far as he or she can, without beginning to tense up or slow down. The minute the youngster feels he or she is starting to tighten up or slow down, then that individual eases off, walks the rest of the lap and then repeats the process. This drill is extremely effective in teaching youngsters to sprint relaxed. I like to put two cones 50 yards apart and time the youngsters for the 50 while they are doing "Whistlers." When we tell them how fast they are running the 50 completely relaxed it has a great impact. If someone is smart enough to figure out this is a running start time, tell that individual there is only a .1 difference between a standing and a running start time. That isn't true, but no one has ever challenged me on that point yet. The key to "Whistlers" is not only to get youngsters to sprint relaxed, but to convince them that they can run faster that way. This drill accomplishes these goals better than any I have ever used.

C. THE MECHANICS OF STARTING TECHNIQUE

1. Block spacing

As a starting point we teach a medium block positioning. The front block is placed a distance from the starting line equal to the distance from the top of the knee to the base of the foot. The back block is set one foot back from the front. This is, of course, only a starting point and an approximation. Every individual is different and, under the supervision of the coach, each youngster should experiment until the most effective block spacing is found for each individual. You have to have some place to start, but never force your preconceived ideas of block spacing on your sprinters. Block spacing must be determined on an individual basis.

When making adjustments a basic rule should be followed. If you increase the spread between the front and rear blocks, bring the front block up closer to the starting line. If you bring the two blocks closer together, place the front block further back. In the former you are moving toward the spread start and in the latter toward the bunch.

2. The mark position

While on the mark, the knee of the rear leg is on the ground, the arms are spread at shoulder width, and the weight is on the finger tips with the thumb and first finger as close to the line as possible. The weight of the body should be shifted slightly forward with the head down and the neck relaxed. Complete concentration and relaxation are essential at this point.

3. The set position

On the command "Set" the athlete raises the buttocks smoothly and quickly into a position that brings the hips just slightly higher than the shoulders and the shoulders out slightly over the starting line. Both legs should be well bent. Pressure should be felt on the finger tips but not to the extent that the sprinter begins to quiver. If the sprinter starts to shake in the set position, there is too much weight forward. If the back leg straightens, the tail is too high. While in the "Set" position the head remains down and every effort should be made to be as relaxed as possible with complete concentration on the gun. (See Figure 4.1.)

FIGURE 4.1 Set Position

4. The takeoff

When the gun goes off the sprinter should drive out low with a vigorous action of the left arm (if the right leg is back). The front or driving leg should obtain full extension before losing contact with the starting block. The rear leg fires out, landing on and driving off the toes. The length of that first stride should be as long as possible provided the knee is out ahead of the ankle and foot when the foot makes contact with the ground. Great care should be taken to observe the first few steps to be sure they are coming straight out of the blocks and not off to the side. (See Figure 4.2.)

FIGURE 4.2   Sprint Takeoff

5. Gaining the full running stride

Coming out of the blocks the sprinter should drive out low, gradually coming up until the full sprinter's stride is reached somewhere between 15–20 yards out. To get the full benefit of the drive out of the blocks, it is very important not to come up too quickly. On the other hand, it is even more important not to stay low too long. A vital coaching point to stress to all sprinters is that the test of a good start is not who gets out of the blocks first, but who is out there in proper sprinting stride running at full speed first. To gain maximum efficiency, an athlete must be in full sprinting stride no further than 20 yards into the race.

D. TRAINING HIGH SCHOOL SPRINTERS

Training sprinters in New England is seriously complicated by weather conditions and the fact that some of our sprinters compete in indoor track while many others are in basketball, playing hockey, etc., and we do not see them until the spring. Everyone has his own unique situation. The important thing is not to push a sprinter all out until he or she has a good running base of cross-country type work and the legs are ready for it. Ideally, a good sprinter should spend the entire fall season working out on alternate days with the cross-country team mixed with weight training and uphill running. Downhill running in the fall is very beneficial, also, but only on good days and only after at least three weeks of conditioning.

I have seldom had a sprinter who wasn't either a football player or soccer player in the fall. Their base training may not be ideal, but we know that they are in shape when they come to us. The same is true of basketball players who come to us in the spring. Hockey players are in good condition but usually take a bit longer getting their "running legs." Regardless of their background, I insist on a minimum of three weeks of base running before moving into our regular sprint training program. Even our indoor runners are given two weeks between seasons and are put on the three week base running program at the beginning of the spring season. This makes good sense in New England because state regulations prohibit the start of spring practice before the second week in March, and March is simply not the time for all-out running in this area.

Once the base work is completed a concerted effort should be made to include each of the sprint drills as often as possible in the weekly training schedule. Obviously, one should not attempt to incorporate all of them on the same day. In this part of the country it is difficult to stick to a predetermined training schedule because there are certain aspects of sprint training that should be avoided on cold, raw, rainy days. It is necessary to set our training schedule in advance and then adjust as weather conditions dictate.

It is our practice to begin each week with a relaxed cross-country run on Sunday following a major Saturday meet. A solid anaerobic workout is a must every week, and, whenever possible, two workouts of this type each week should be included. Our basic anaerobic workout involves 6 × 330's at 90 percent effort with roughly 5 minutes rest between repetitions. You can vary the distance and repetitions in this type of workout, as long as the workout forces the athlete to run in oxygen debt and is building resistance to lactic acid formation.

Whistlers are particularly effective with sprinters as are sprint-float-sprint 120's. In the latter workout the sprinter drives out of the blocks into full running stride for 40 yards, there is then an easing off to a very relaxed 50% in the middle 40, and then full out again the final 40 yards to the finish line concentrating on relaxation and a good lean into the tape.

I try to work on some relay passing at least three times a week and practice starts at least twice. When practicing starts for technique, sprinters should take the starts alone. Technique starts involving more than one sprinter at a time, unless there is a coach or critic for each individual, result in a lack of constructive criticism and analysis as it is impossible to watch more than one person at a time. Technique starts should not be at full speed as the sprinter should be thinking of technique and not thinking of exploding out of the blocks as is the case when in competition.

All starting work full out should be highly competitive. A sprinter should never go up against opposition without the competitive determination to be first. Also, competitive starts should be at a minimum of 30 yards so that everyone has come out of the blocks and into full sprinting stride properly. Competitive starts at shorter distances tend to induce the athletes to stay low too long. Competitive starts at 10–15–20 yards tend to be 10–15–20 yard races and are counter-productive to good sprinting technique.

Good starting technique is only half the battle. Good sprinters must have fast natural reaction to sound. Ask your sprinters at what point does the realization come to them that the race is under way. A youngster with fast reactions will not realize the race is underway until he or she is several steps out of the blocks. Individuals with slow reactions recognize the race has started while still in the blocks. The great ones explode with the gun rather than run as a result of hearing it. When a sprinter gets a super start, he or she is often half-expecting to get the second gun.

It is debatable whether or not you can increase an individual's reactions to sound. One thing is certain, you must insist on complete quiet and eliminate all distractions when working on starting. Also, you cannot improve something if you do not practice it. This is a major reason why all gun starts should be highly competitive.

Strength and flexibility are absolute essentials to good sprinting. Sprinters should be on a year-round strength and flexibility program. In the off-season our sprinters work on a three-day-per-week schedule utilizing the regular workout concept described in Chapter 2. Once the competitive season begins we cut back to twice a week utilizing the regular-explosive sequence and never lifting the day prior to competition. With many sprinters it is a good idea to avoid this type of work two days before a major meet or serious challenge. We utilize the weight machine with all our runners rather than the free weights because of our numbers, facilities and equipment. I have no argument with the use of free weights in these areas, however. We do insist upon squats with the free weights for all our sprinters and hurdlers and avoid the leg press on the machine with all runners.

Weight machine workout:

Bench press	Inclined sit-ups
Military press	Leg lifts
Forearm curls	Heel raises (Free weights)
Upright rowing	Squats (Free weights)
Kneeling pulldowns	Leg extensions
Trunk twists	Leg curls
Dips	

In addition to decreasing the chances of injury, the more flexible the individual, the easier it is to develop proper stride length and leg speed. In addition to the regular flexibility exercises before every practice and competition, all runners would do well to make a practice of taking 10 minutes in the morning and 10 minutes before they go to bed to repeat this stretching work.

E. PSYCHOLOGICAL ASPECTS OF SPRINTING

1. The sprinter's ego

If a youngster is not something of an egotist regarding his or her ability to run fast, then that individual is probably not going to reach the pinnacle. There is something unique about being the fastest kid on the block, or the fastest athlete on the team or in the state etc.. Cultivate this in your sprinters. I don't mean encouraging them to be boastful or conceited, but work on their pride. Competitive instinct is essential to success in all athletic areas, but it is particularly vital in sprinting because of the extreme intensity and shortness of competitive duration of a sprinting event.

2. Dealing with nervous tension

Nervous tension can be both good and bad for a sprinter. Most good sprinters tend to be high-strung individuals. To some degree this is due to their competitive intensity and the ego factor just described. High-strung people tend to have quick reactions, and this, of course, is desirable in sprinting. Nevertheless, relaxation is the key to sprinting success and the coach must work to avoid tension in sprinters prior to competition. Sprinters are excruciatingly aware that one mistake more often than not will cost them a race and this leads to great nervousness. Also, most sprinters have a great fear that the speed will just not be there. One has to have been a sprinter to really appreciate this, but there definitely are times the looseness isn't present, or tightening takes place and the great explosiveness that all sprinters look for is missing. This is a very intangible thing. One may just call it that extra fine edge, but anyone who has ever sprinted knows what I am talking about. The end result is that it produces a very jumpy athlete come race time. It is a vitally important role of the coach to keep sprinters as calm, relaxed and confident as possible before race time. This, of course, is an aspect of coaching applicable to all events, but, in my judgment, a little more so in dealing with sprinters.

3. End of the race psychology

Even in a race as short as 100 yards, the individual who appears to be going the fastest at the end of the race is actually the individual who is slowing down the least. Tests have proved that speed stops increasing after the first 60 yards, after which the task is to prevent slowing down. This involves good form and relaxation because the natural tendency is to strain to go faster and this, of course, increases the slowing down process. It takes a great deal of work and concentration to overcome this tendency because it is such a natural one. Sprint races are often lost psychologically rather than through any physical inferiority because the loser tried too hard at the end to increase speed and succeeded in tying up instead. Sprinters must be trained to do just the opposite of what their natural reactions or instincts tell them to do at the end of the race. I particularly recommend the Whistlers Drill as a device to accomplish this and also as a means of convincing athletes on the value and necessity of relaxed sprinting.

F. SPECIAL PROBLEMS IN COACHING GIRL SPRINTERS

Everything is relative in sprinting and we do not train the girls any differently from the boys. There are a few factors to consider, however, one of them being upper body strength. This is an extremely vital area in sprinting and, since girls do not have the same strength as boys, considerable attention must be devoted to it. We put the girls on the weights the same as the boys, but if facilities or a particular girl's reluctance becomes a problem, push-ups, sit-ups, chin-ups and leg lifts on a regular basis can be very beneficial. Many high school girl sprinters are simply not going to get involved in increasing upper body strength and if you give definite attention to it you are going to gain an edge for your girl sprinters.

In sprinting, girls have more of a tendency to carry their elbows away from their bodies than do the boys, particularly if they have some degree of bust development. As a result, many girls have an arm action that tends to come across the body rather than forward and back. This is a problem that can be corrected and careful attention should be given to it. We put a great deal of emphasis upon our arm action drills with all our sprinters, but particularly with the girls.

Many girl sprinters tend to mature more quickly than the boys and also tend to begin to lose their speed due to body development at an earlier age. Look for potential girls sprinters early, certainly no later than when they first hit junior high. Also, stress the importance of good dieting habits. If you can hold the weight down, you might well get that extra year or two before a decline begins to set in.

G. COACHING THE SPRINT RELAYS

Most great sprint relay teams use the overhand pass and pass right to left, left to right, and right to left. We use the underhand pass and make all passes right to left for three important reasons: (1) indoor track, (2) the large number of relay events scheduled during the season, and (3) the limitations on participation in Massachusetts rules. In indoor track relay passes are always made on a turn or coming off a turn. Passing from left to right becomes very awkward in such conditions. In Massachusetts we compete in State Relay championships involving seven races in both indoor and outdoor track, as well as several invitationals where as many as four relay events are run. Further, in Massachusetts an individual is limited to two running events in all meets, including relays. In dual meets, however, we can double a runner in individual events but in major meets the rules allow only one individual running event and one relay. These conditions necessitate considerable juggling of relay teams. We teach one pass to every member of the squad. No matter how we juggle members of relay teams, although the timing will, of course, be different, the passing technique is always the same.

We use the right-to-left technique because of indoor track and because you also get some curve passing during the outdoor season. We use the underhand pass because it is a little more natural, and easier to teach every member of the squad. With the underhand pass you must get 6″–1′ closer to make the exchange and you create a slight disadvantage by two runners switching hands. I am, convinced, however, that these disadvantages are more than made up for in the consistency we gain. If you are coaching in a warm weather area that does not compete in indoor track, and if you can count on running the same foursome all season, then the overhand—alternating exchanges are to your advantage. If your conditions are similar to those we face in Massachusetts, however, then you are well advised to consider teaching one system, to sprinters and distance runners alike, and sticking to it.

In utilizing the underhand pass the outgoing runner should pump the arms in sprinting action for four or five strides then place the left hand palm down directly to the left side, reaching back about 18″ behind the left hip. Care should be taken to keep the thumb and fingers relaxed but firm and parallel to the line of run. It is very important that the thumb and fingers not be perpendicular to the line of run and thus obstruct the pass into the palm of the hand. Be sure also that the hand is cupped and the palm down. The palm must not be turned upward if a maximum target is to be presented. The incoming runner places the baton in the palm of the outgoing runner with an upward swing deviating from proper sprinting arm action as little as possible. (See Figure 4.3.)

Regardless of the passing technique used, the real key to success in the sprint relays is timing. The pass must be made at the exact moment that the speed of the outgoing runner reaches that of the athlete coming in. The baton must not slow down. The fact that you can get the baton to the outgoing runner a bit quicker with the overhand pass does not mean you have made a better exchange. It is the speed of the baton that counts. A perfect pass can be made with any technique. Select the passing technique that you feel, given your particular conditions, best facilitates the timing of the exchange.

Practicing sprint relay passing is one of the most difficult aspects of track and field. Working on exchanging technique is easy, working on timing is something else again. If you do not simulate exact speed and fatigue conditions, your passing practice may well be counter-productive. Actually, the only way to simulate competitive conditions is to work at full race distances. The problem with this is how often can you do it this way without disrupting your regular sprinting workouts and how often can you work at full distance on a given day and still be as fresh as during

FIGURE 4.3   Right-to-Left Underhand Pass

competition. Further, no matter how fresh the athletes may be in practice, the adrenaline of competition is missing.

I feel you have to compromise on this issue. Some days we will run the full distance just once. One good pass at meet conditions is better than a dozen passes at speeds that may throw off timing. On days when we feel we want to get in a little more passing work, we run the full distance exchanging at full tilt, but slowing down to about half-speed for the middle 60 yards of each 110 leg. This is not perfect, but it comes as close as you can to simulating actual conditions without running the full race. The worst thing anyone can do is to try to combine a conditioning workout with relay passing. The practice of putting five youngsters on the track and running three or four laps of consecutive 110 relay exchanges may be a great workout, but certainly is destructive to timing.

I believe in both a visual and verbal takeoff. The receiver should be looking over the shoulder and know exactly when the incoming runner reaches the takeoff point. The receiver takes off, however, only upon the verbal command. A blind takeoff may be theoretically faster but never in the confusion of competition. The last thing in the world you want is a runner taking off on someone else's command.

The exchange, of course, should be made blind in all sprint relays. The outgoing runner should take off at full speed with full sprinting arm action. Only at a second verbal command from the incoming runner should the exchange position of the receiver's arm be established.

1. The most common faults in relay passing

(1) The receiver does not take off at full speed.

(2) The incoming runner slows down just as he or she reaches the outgoing runner. This is psychologically an instinctive thing to do. The problem is that the outgoing runner is gaining speed on every step. Coaches must constantly stress that the incoming runner not slow down until the outgoing runner has the baton and is safely underway.

(3) The outgoing runner jumps the gun and takes off too soon.

(4) The outgoing runner grabs for the baton and does not hold the target steady.

(5) The incoming runner takes his or her eyes off the target and slaps the baton, missing the exchange. I always tell my runners it is just like playing golf, keep your eye on the ball.

(6) The outgoing runner does not hug the inside of the lane and the incoming runner does not favor the outside of the lane. If this happens you will get one runner running up the other's back. The baton exchange itself should be made in the center of the lane.

2. Placement of personnel on the sprint relay team

There is no such thing as an ideal order in placing runners on your relay team. No four individuals have exactly the same characteristics. What you have to do is to analyze carefully the people you have and base your placement on the best combination of factors. Below are the major considerations that should go into this analysis.

(1) If you have an individual who is particularly strong coming out of the blocks, consider that individual, naturally, for the lead-off position.

(2) Your strongest runner and best competitor makes the best anchor.

(3) If you have individuals who are excellent passers, take advantage of their passing ability and run them either second or third.

(4) If you have a runner who is a decent starter but has trouble receiving, consider running that individual lead-off.

(5) If you have a runner with difficulty handing off, consider that individual as the anchor.

(6) If an individual is a good curve runner, consider that person for legs one or three. Good straightaway runners are best utilized on legs two and four. This factor only applies when the 4 × 110 is run utilizing the full straightaway at the finish.

(7) If you have a very strong runner at 120 yards consider running this individual second. By taking a full fly zone when that individual is receiving and by taking no fly zone when he or she is handing off, you can gain at least an extra 15 yards in the distance that individual runs. The best you can add to the anchor's distance is half that if you take the full fly zone. The best you can add to the lead-off is also half of what you can add to the second leg if you take no fly zone.

(8) If you have a particularly weak runner, consider running that individual third. If he or she takes no fly zone receiving and hands off to the anchor with a full fly zone, you can cut off at least 15 yards on the distance that individual runs.

2. The fly zone

The fly zone should not be used as a crutch for increasing the passing zone. Twenty meters is plenty of room to make an efficient pass. The determination on whether or not to use a fly zone should be based upon altering the distances your athletes will run in order to best utilize your personnel. If my best sprinter is also an extremely proficient passer, I like to run that individual second and have done so on some of my state championship sprint relay teams. You could get the same effect running him third but that would cut down on the anchor leg.

SAMPLE SPRINTERS WORK WEEK (MID-SEASON)

<u>Monday:</u>

30 Min. Flexibility and warm-up
15 Min. 10 × Downhill running
60 Min. 6 × 330's 90 percent Anaerobic

Advanced	Beginners
45 Min. Regular weight workout	15 Min. 10 × Uphill running

SAMPLE SPRINTERS WORK WEEK (MID-SEASON) *(Continued)*

Tuesday:

30 Min. Flexibility and warm-up
10 Min. Sprint drills
30 Min. Gun starts

Advanced	Beginners
20 Min. Relay passing	15 Min. 10 × Uphill running
15 Min. Weight jacket running	45 Min. Regular weight workout
15 Min. 10 × Uphill running	

Wednesday:

30 Min. Flexibility and warm-up
15 Min. 10 × downhill running
20 Min. 4 × 120's (Start-coast-finish)
15 Min. All out 300 yard run

Advanced	Beginners
15 Min. 10 × Uphill running	15 Min. Weight jacket running
45 Min. Explosive weight workout	30 Min. Relay passing drills

Thursday:

30 Min. Flexibility and warm-up
10 Min. Sprint drills
20 Min. Gun starts
30 Min. 6 × Whistlers (relaxation
          sprinting

Advanced	Beginners
30 Min. Relay passing	45 Min. Explosive weight workout

Friday:

Rest or optional light loosening workout

Saturday:

Competition

Goal day for beginners on Friday if not running Saturday

Sunday:

Easy relaxed 3 miles on own

CHAPTER 5

COACHING THE DISTANCE AND MIDDLE-DISTANCE RUNNERS

A. RUNNING TECHNIQUE

Running is the most natural of athletic activities. There is little point in making a youngster think more than is necessary in doing something as instinctive as running. We stress only two points to our beginners before their first workout. The two basic fundamentals of running are relaxation and keeping the body in a straight line. Anything an individual does that reduces relaxation and leads to tightening up is wrong. Anything that takes the body out of a straight line—(Bobbing the head, twisting the shoulders, swinging the arms from side to side, etc.) also greatly decreases running efficiency. This is all we tell our beginners; remember these two basic fundamentals and then do what comes naturally.

This is not meant to imply that there is no more to running technique. After stressing the two basic fundamentals, we simply observe a runner's natural style and make corrections where necessary. There is no point in coaching something individuals already do naturally. The more you make them think, the harder it is going to be for them to relax. When faults are present, however, they must be corrected. Sometimes pointing out a fault and stressing proper technique is all that is needed. If this is not sufficient, then take the individuals aside and directly work on technique. Let them run as naturally as they can, but don't fill their heads with your expertise if it isn't necessary.

In checking running technique, look for the following:

1. Relaxation

As with the sprinters, stress keeping the jaw and the hands loose. Think of running from the hips down.

2. Head carriage

Be sure the head is level. If the youngster has a tendency to throw the head back this has a definite tightening effect and also cuts off the air supply. If the head is down, there will be a tendency to run hunched over, and looking at the ground often leads to falling on one's face. Be sure, also, the head is still and not bobbing from side to side. A good coaching point is to emphasize—run the way you walk.

3. Arm carriage

The arms should be carried low at roughly the belt level. Carrying the arms too high has a serious tightening effect. If they are carried too low, literally at the sides, then the runner is not going to gain any benefit from arm action.

4. Arm action

The elbows must be kept close to the body so that the arm action is essentially forward and back and not side to side. Be sure the fingers, hands, arms and shoulders are all relaxed.

5. Trunk carriage

Be sure the shoulders are square to the line of run. Don't allow any twisting or turning of the upper body.

6. Center of gravity

Essentially a runner should be erect with the legs directly under the trunk. Sprinters and quarter milers may have a very slight body lean, but basically it is very important to keep the center of gravity directly over the legs.

7. Foot placement

Look for a ball-of-the-foot landing with a rocker-like action of the foot. If the youngster is banging the heels first, running flat-footed or running entirely up on the toes, these faults must be corrected.

8. Stride length

There is no such thing as an ideal stride length. What may be perfect for one individual may be fatal to another. Clearly, however, some youngsters overstride while others run with steps that are much too short and choppy. It is your role to recommend a lengthening or shortening of an athlete's stride if you determine it is necessary. Ideally, you are looking for a stride length with which the youngster is most confident and comfortable and which you feel results in maximum running efficiency.

I believe that if you want to cure a serious problem in running technique, that should be the sole objective of that phase of the practice session. Do not attempt to correct running style during a regular workout. The youngster will be much more concerned with the nature and quality of the workout, or with just being able to finish it, than he or she will be with altering technique. This is a lesson learned from 28 years of coaching—never try to accomplish two objectives in one drill. If technique alteration is your goal, take the youngster aside and just stride easily the length of the football field, resting or walking back after each run-through. Keep on repeating the process, giving the youngster nothing to think about or worry about other than his or her technique. Set aside 15 minutes a day for this or, if necessary, devote the entire practice session to it. If on a given day you can make an individual a more efficient runner, you have gained infinitely more than what may be lost by not getting in the scheduled workout for that day.

B. TRAINING THE DISTANCE AND MIDDLE DISTANCE RUNNERS

1. Milers and two milers

Although at higher levels the mile and two mile are considered middle distance, at the high school level these are our distance people. The training of any runner is an individual matter. What may be a fine training program for one athlete may well not be for another. Don't try to copy the programs of the great runners. It may be great for them on the international level, but most of us will never be lucky enough to work with people even close to that caliber. Set your training program to fit your own particular circumstances and the needs of your runners.

Regardless of how a running program is organized, it should consist of five basic types of workouts: (1) aerobic long-distance running, (2) interval work, (3) anaerobic repeat work, (4) pace work, and (5) sprint work. The bulk portion of each workout should involve either 1–2 or 3 or a combination; 4 and 5 are worked in along with the bulk workout.

(1) Aerobic long-distance work

We like to hit the roads every other day in the early season and a minimum of twice a week during competition. Hitting the roads is actually just a figure of speech. Running through the woods, fields or over a golf course is much less demanding on the legs than pounding the macadam. In New England, however, weather conditions during a good part of the year give one very little choice and a good part of our long-distance running actually is road running.

Our distance coach just completed his 20th Boston Marathon at the age of fifty. This is a great advantage because he goes right out and runs with our distance people. The great ones are no problem, but if you have to send high school runners out on a long-distance run unsupervised, you can bet some are just going to plod along and get very little out of it. Years ago when I coached the entire team all by myself I would send some out and others I kept within my vision. I know it is easy to say that if you can't trust them to work hard on their own they never will be any good anyway, but that just isn't true. A youngster who has to be supervised and pushed all the time will never be a great champion, but that type of individual can still be a definite asset to your team.

Be sure to vary your long-distance workouts. Having a coach out there with the runners is a great asset in that regard. Take them out to different areas of town and vary the distances run and the pace of the run. During a given long-distance workout at times include some hill running. Have them pick up the pace for periods of varying length or time and then ease off again. We have our telephone pole drills where the runners will pick up the pace for two or three telephone poles and then settle back again. Marathon runners have what they call the Three-Minute Drill where they pick up the pace considerably for a three-minute period. One might call this sort of thing directed Fartlek. This type of long-distance training should be mixed in with steady running over a prescribed distance.

(2) Interval work

This type of workout is a must once a week and at times, when the competitive load is not heavy we will attempt to run intervals on a twice-weekly basis. Some coaches do solely long-distance training and others concentrate strictly on intervals. Most good ones that I know utilize both and we are sold on that concept. We have established repeat 440's as our basic interval distance, but there is nothing sacred about the 440 and once in a while we will run intervals at other distances (660–880, etc.) for variety.

The value of this type of workout comes from the run-recover-run-recover, etc. cycle. The ideal method is to test the pulse rate of each individual after every interval run to be sure the athlete has recovered sufficiently to repeat the run again. For the average person that means getting the pulse rate back to 120. If you can do this properly, fine, but I have great doubts about the accuracy of young athletes getting a correct pulse reading over and over again during a strenuous workout.

The system we use is not unique, but it is more practical and it is effective. Our intervals are done at a pace the athlete can sustain for ten minutes. Basically we set up the intervals based upon what we judge that individual ought to be able to run a two mile. A 9:20 two miler would run at 70 seconds for the 440, the 10:00 man at 75 seconds, etc. The interval of recovery is equal to the time of the run. Those running :70 would use :70 recovery, those running at :90 would have a :90 recovery time. This is just a rule of thumb, however. If a youngster cannot handle the workout with the recovery time allowed, then you must either give him more time to recover or put him in a slower-paced group. This type of workout is of little value if a youngster cannot accomplish it successfully.

It is very important to make these interval workouts progressive. We start off the season at 10 × 440 and work up from there. I have had some good runners who could run 20 × 440 by the end of the season. The other progressive alternative is to reduce the recovery time rather than the number of repetitions—quality vs. quantity. Either system is effective as long as progression exists and the youngsters can successfully complete the workouts.

A controversial factor in interval running among coaches is what should be done during the recovery period. No less an authority than Jim Ryun says it doesn't really make any difference. Some like to jog, some like to walk, some like to stretch and some even do exercises. I believe it is important to keep moving and not lie or sit down during the recovery period. Our system of equal run and recovery periods is based upon walking in between runs. If you have your athletes jog, they will probably require a slightly longer recovery period. Obviously, the more you do during the recovery period, the longer it is going to take to get the pulse rate down. The key is not to make the recovery period any longer than necessary, but, even more important make it long enough.

(3) Anaerobic repeat work

Anaerobic work is essential in a distance running program. Regardless of the distance an individual is running, at some point toward the end of a competitive race the athlete is going to experience oxygen debt and the resulting lactic acid formation. It is necessary to develop a resistance to this lactic acid with a type of training that puts the runner in oxygen debt. Further, this type of training is a quality workout with the athlete running at faster-than-race pace. Our basic anaerobic workout distance is 330 yards but again there is nothing sacred about that distance. Repeats at 220, 440 or ladder-type workouts are also very effective. We run our anaerobic workout at 90 percent of an individual's best time for the distance, taking only that amount of time between repetitions necessary to get the job done. Five minutes between runs is a good rule of thumb to follow, but do not push a youngster at that rate if he or she cannot handle it. On the other hand, if that long a rest is not needed, don't use the full five minutes. The important thing is for the athlete to be able to perform the workout successfully. If we really want to push our runners, we will give them eight repetitions, more often we will run six, and even on some days four if we want to add something else in the workout.

(4) Pace work

Every full work day we will use one of the three previously described types of workouts, or a combination thereof, as the bulk part of the practice. If you are going to work on pace, put that phase of the workout right after the warm-up when the youngsters are still fresh. We have them run three or four 220's at the pace desired for their particular race. Have them run into the start, run through a 220, time them and give them the time immediately. Let them rest a couple of minutes and run them through again. By trial and error the athletes will get the feel of the pace you want them to run.

You can talk all you want to your runners about running at a

70-second-per-quarter pace, for example, but if they have never actually run at that pace, how can they be expected to achieve it? I feel, just as in teaching technique, if the goal is to teach pace, don't try to accomplish it as part of an aerobic or anaerobic workout. Don't try to accomplish two things at once when learning is an objective. Once a runner has a good concept of pace this type of workout is not necessary except once every week or two just as a refresher. For those individuals who have real problems with pace it is worth devoting a brief 15-minute segment at the beginning of practice as often as possible.

(5) Sprint work

Regardless of the distance at which a runner is competing, even if it be a marathon, it is a foot race and the person with the greatest amount of sprint speed, all other factors being equal, is the one who is going to be the winner. We put a 15-minute segment of sprinting work into every practice when feasible. Every runner needs sprint work; nobody can run fast enough.

It is important not to equate what many refer to as speed work with what I refer to here as sprinting work. Running 330's, 440's, 660's etc. at faster-than-race pace is quality work and plays a vital role in an athlete's training, but it is not designed to build pure speed. Every day that weather conditions and the physical state of the athlete permit, we give our distance runners 15 minutes of the same type of work we give our sprinters. This entails downhill running, uphill running, and particularly, the "Whistlers" described in the chapter on sprinting. This involves starting off slowly in the middle of the curve, coming off the curve at full speed, concentrating on good form and relaxation, and holding that speed until the athlete feels himself or herself beginning to slow down and tighten up. When they feel this tightening or slowing down, they ease off, walk the rest of the lap, and repeat the process. These "Whistlers" can be run at the beginning or end of a practice session. I particularly like to give our distance runners six "Whistlers" at the end of a workout as there is a great deal of merit in acquainting runners with sprinting relaxed and in good form when tired. After all, this is the bottom line in any foot race.

(6) Twice-a-day workouts

Working out twice a day is basic among the great ones. If you can get your distance runners to run a long, slow distance early in the morning and then come back for the day's regular workout after school, you are going to be that much ahead of the game. We just do not feel we can push this sort of thing, although we certainly encourage it, because some of our youngsters have to be out at the bus stop prior to 7:00 A.M. in the morning. I am not about to take on the mothers of the community on this one. If you do have individuals working on a twice-a-day schedule, be sure to monitor it very closely. If they cannot handle the regular workouts as a result, you should probably consider eliminating the morning runs, at least for a while. More may be, but is not necessarily, better. It is easy to overwork or burn out a good runner.

2. Training quarter-milers

Although we classify quarter-milers as middle distance, essentially they are sprinters who need a great deal of endurance. Quarter-milers should hit the roads with the distance runners two or three times a week in the pre-competitive season and at least once a week in the competitive part of the schedule. Over-distance work is also vital for quarter-milers at the high school level, not only for the endurance factor, but psychologically to give the athlete confidence at the 440 distance. This is extremely important for quarter-milers who are the most prone of all runners to running out of gas or hitting that stonewall. At least once a week we like to give our quarter-milers repeat 660's or 880's.

Since the quarter miler is the most prone to oxygen debt, anaerobic work is a must and we attempt to incorporate this type of work twice a week into our schedule whenever possible. Six repeat 330's at 90 percent with roughly five minutes rest is an excellent anaerobic workout for quarter-milers.

Since quarter-milers are essentially sprinters, they must train as sprinters. Quarter-milers should do starting work, downhill and uphill running, "Whistlers" and all the other sprint drills described in the sprinting chapter. They won't get as much of this type of work as the sprinters because of the endurance and anaerobic work in their program, but I feel a quarter-miler's program should be basically one-third endurance, one-third anaerobic and one-third sprinting work.

There is no event where sprinting relaxed and in good form is more essential than in the quarter mile. We have two drills we use that are beneficial in this area both in building the ability to sprint relaxed and in good form when tired and also to build confidence in not running out of gas or hitting the stonewall. We have our athletes run the first 660 of an 880 yard run at 2:40 speed running the last 220 of the 880 just as if running the final 220 of a quarter mile concentrating again on relaxation and good form. We have them run three of these in a given workout. We will also have them run a one mile slightly faster than a jog coming off the final corner on each of the four laps as though they were running through the tape in a 440. In any drill of this nature it is essential for the quarter-miler to understand that everybody slows down at the end of the quarter and the goal is to keep relaxed and in good form in order to be the one who slows down the least.

3. Training the half-milers

The half mile is the legitimate middle-distance race. It isn't a sprint, but it is run much too rapidly to be considered a distance run either. Basically we train our half-milers with our milers and two-milers and all three events come under our distance coach in our staff organization. They do all their long-distance endurance work and intervals with our distance runners, but they just do not do quite as much of it. Half milers need more anaerobic and sprinting work than do the milers and two-milers. We try to set a policy of 50 percent endurance or aerobic work, 35 percent anaerobic and 15 percent sprint work in our half-mile training program. We will also put our half-milers through the same type of finish work as we give the quarter-milers.

4. Strength training for distance and middle-distance runners

Upper and middle body strength is essential in all areas of track and field and is particularly important for all runners. Our quarter-milers are trained by the sprint coach and are put on a regular weight training program just as the sprinters. Our basic weight program for sprinters and quarter-milers is described in Chapter 2. If we have a really outstanding distance runner we encourage that individual to go on the weights also. Our weight training facilities and the numbers we have on the squad simply prohibit their use by everybody. As a result, our distance coach works his runners faithfully on push-ups, sit-ups, chin-ups and leg lifts to increase upper and middle body strength. If you have the facilities, put all your runners on the weights three times a week during the pre-competitive period and twice a week during competition.

5. Establishing an individualized training program

Although there is no way you can get away from training runners in groups, you should never lose sight of the fact that runners should be trained as much as possible on an individual basis. There is no one training schedule that is ideal for all your runners. Although sample schedules are presented in this chapter, it may well not be the program for a number of our runners. It is your role to find the combination of workouts, employing the basic principles outlined, that best suits each individual. No two runners are exactly alike and no two runners have exactly the same needs. The key is not to neglect any of the basic areas of training and to place the emphasis where it best meets the needs of each individual.

In setting up an individualized program, three basic factors should be kept in mind.

(1) What does the individual need?

Emphasis should be given in each program to an individual's weaknesses. This does not mean that any area of training should be neglected; it simply means organizing a training schedule designed to improve a runner where that individual needs it the most.

(2) What can the individual handle?

It is a grave mistake to set up a program that is too tough for a particular individual and results in that youngster's failure to complete the workout prescribed. Psychologically, a workout that ends in failure can be very damaging. If you assign an athlete a workout of 16 interval quarters as an example and he falls apart on the 14th, stumbling through 15 and 16, the day's work may well be counter-productive. It is far better to have completed 13 quarters and finish on a high note, than to carry the workout into exhaustion and failure. Certainly this is true psychologically, and I am inclined to believe physically as well. The coach must take great care not to assign workouts that are too difficult and must also know when to cut a workout short in order to avoid failure. This represents a dilemma as very few athletes do not have to be pushed, but care must be taken not to push them too far. There is no secret to this, the skill comes from experience. A major key to successful coaching is the ability to push athletes to the limit, but not beyond that limit.

(3) What does the athlete perceive as his needs?

Don't minimize the importance of discussing a runner's training program with him. The athlete has to run the race, not you. If a particular youngster feels he needs more speed work, or more long distance, or whatever, give it to him as long as you still incorporate all the various aspects of training and still provide him with a balanced and solid program. If an extra day out on the roads, for example, gives a runner confidence, then by all means see that he gets it. A confident athlete, satisfied with his training program is definitely going to perform better for you.

6. Running strategy

Planning strategy in a distance or middle-distance race can often do more harm than good. Unless you are dealing with a strong, confident runner, and unless you are really knowledgeable regarding the strengths and weaknesses of the opposition, you may well hurt your runner by filling his or her head with all kinds of racing tactics. Basic strategy should involve getting clear of the pack to avoid getting bounced around at the start, settling into a pace mutually agreed upon for that race and keeping it consistent throughout, finally kicking from a point at which the individual is confident, concentrating on good form and relaxation. If that doesn't win so be it, the youngster has given his or her best.

With a strong, confident runner, by all means take advantage of known weaknesses in the opposition. If you can demoralize opponents with an early fast pace, set one. If they tend to give up if you pick up the pace at some point in the race, then pick it up. If you know you can outkick an individual, hang on his shoulder and let him do the work. There are all kinds of weaknesses that can be exploited to a good runner's advantage. Be careful, however, not to destroy your own runner's continuity by getting cute with tactics, and don't fool around against a superior runner. In most cases, and certainly with beginners, the best strategy you can use is tell them to run their own race.

With quarter-milers particularly, the concept of running one's own race makes the greatest sense. A quarter-miler should get out and run the first 220 within 1–2 seconds of top 220 time. What you shoot for depends on that individual's ability to handle it, but if a youngster is running the first 220 slower than two seconds of maximum effort, that individual is not going to beat many good quarter-milers. After the first 220, the quarter-miler attempts to continue that pace as long as he or she can, concentrating on good form and relaxation and keeping slowing down to a minimum. There really are no racing tactics among top-notch quarter-milers, it is essentially a sprint race.

C. THE TWO KEY PSYCHOLOGICAL ASPECTS OF DISTANCE AND MIDDLE-DISTANCE RUNNING

1. The fear of running out of gas

By far the greatest psychological phenomenon with which we have to deal in running is the fear of running out of gas. Most runners at the high school level have a fear of looking bad and falling apart at the end of a race that is much more intense than any fear of losing. This is most often demonstrated by what we call the "¾ syndrome." How often do we see a youngster pull back and slacken the pace somewhere between the midpoint and the ¾ point of a race. A 4:40 miler, for example runs splits of 70–70–75–65. Why did the runner fall back to :75 in the third quarter. Obviously, it was not a physical factor. If he was forced physically back to :75 in the third quarter of the race, there is no way in the world he is going to come back with a :65 final quarter. What happened was the youngster fell back because he did not feel confident that he could finish strong maintaining the original pace.

This is an extremely common problem with beginners and even with many so-called experienced runners. You have to convince your athletes that they can maintain a steady predetermined pace throughout the race, and make it clear how unhappy you are going to be with them if they do not. With certain types of youngsters it can be very effective if you can make their fear of your unhappiness stronger than their fear of running out of gas.

I do not care how bad a runner looks in the final quarter of a race, I shower that individual with praise if he or she has run a steady, consistent pace for the first three quarters, even if the end result is running out of gas. There is no way a youngster can ever run a steady pace the entire race if he or she never tries it. If you have predetermined a pace that is not unreasonable for that individual, there is no reason in the world why it cannot be accomplished. The key is to sell the youngster that based upon the quality of his or her workouts it definitely can be done. If it just cannot be done physically, then you have set too fast a pace for that youngster and should cut it down a bit.

In developing an even pace, it is a good coaching tactic to check times at a point other than at the finish line. In every race there is a run for position at the beginning. It is very doubtful that even an all-out sprint the first 50 or 60 yards of a race is going to have any adverse effect upon overall performance. Consequently, the first lap time may not be indicative of the actual pace being run. Checking lap times at the midpoint of the back stretch, or at the end of the first 220, makes more sense. Also, giving lap times may be fine for experienced runners, but it can often be fatal for beginners. How often do we see runners fall apart when they hear a time called off they feel is too fast. As said before, the time may very well not represent the actual pace being currently run. Further, if someone else gives it, who is to say it is accurate? I tell my runners not to pay attention to anything they hear unless it is from me or the distance coach. We never give them their times during a race; the analysis will come afterwards. We simply holler, "you're doing fine," "Pick it up just a little," or "relax you are just a bit fast"—the latter when they are definitely going too fast. The last thing we want a youngster to do is panic in the middle of a race. For the most part, what they don't know won't hurt them.

2. Trying too hard

Equally important is the need to overcome the psychological urge to try harder when greater speed is needed. This will come when attempting to ward off a challenge, or in the race to the tape. You must sell all runners that relaxation and good running technique make an individual run faster, not straining at the bit. You must impress upon your runners that if they are going as fast as they can and someone goes by them, there is nothing that can be done about it. Trying to get more speed out of the engine when that speed just isn't there is only going to burn the engine out. The end result is running into the proverbial stonewall. This is why it is necessary to emphasize relaxed sprinting, especially when tired, in the training program.

D. SPECIAL PROBLEMS IN COACHING GIRL DISTANCE AND MIDDLE-DISTANCE RUNNERS

Probably the area in track and field where there is little or no gap between girls and boys, assuming comparable levels of experience and training, is endurance. Don't baby a top-notch girl distance runner. There are four factors to be considered, however. The amount of time spent in a distance run must be considered as well as the amount of territory covered. If you send two individuals out on a ten-mile run and both expend the same degree of effort, the superior runner who runs the distance in say 60 minutes has not taken the pounding that a youngster who ran it in 75 minutes has taken. You are not necessarily babying your girls if you send them out on an 8-mile run while you have assigned the boys 10. Obviously, this is a factor to consider in dealing with inferior male distance runners as well.

I am no expert on female monthly problems and apparently this does not present an obstacle for many girl athletes. For some it does, however, and it can be a factor in a girl's ability to perform. As has been previously discussed, it is vitally important that athletes successfully complete their assigned workouts and breaking down is a condition that must be avoided. Some girls are more prone to this than others and it is a matter to which the coach should give serious attention. The more open the communication between the coach and the athlete on these matters, the better.

In dealing with girls, you will encounter a far greater physical gap between the well-established female athlete and the novice with little athletic background than you will with the boys. There are very extensive youth athletic programs for boys and most come out for track with years of some kind of athletic activity behind them. For a lot of girls this has not been the case. Times are changing rapidly, fortunately, and there may come a time when this condition will no longer exist. It is with us now, however, and many girls are going to come out for a high school track team unable to take the intense training program a coach might think they should have. In no area is this a more significant factor than in distance running. It is extremely vital for the coach to have knowledge of the athletic background of all team members, especially the girls, and to bring those who are not ready for intense training along slowly. It is very easy to wreck a novice girl physically and destroy her psychologically if she is pushed too quickly. Our culture being what it is, there are more girls out there with talent who are not aware of it than boys. Don't push this type too soon. I said you should never baby a top-notch girl runner, or any female athlete for that matter, but baby the novices a little until you are sure they are ready. It may be the difference between making and breaking a fine talent for you some day.

Finally, as with all running and jumping events, weight control is vitally important with female middle and distance runners. Obviously, it is important with the boys also, but girls have to deal with it sooner and more extensively than the boys. Fortunately, a vigorous running program is going to burn off the calories pretty well, but good dieting habits are still essential.

SAMPLE 440 WORK WEEK (MID-SEASON)

Monday:

30 Min. Flexibility and warm-up
15 Min. 10 × downhill running
30 Min. 2 × 880—10 sec. above max.)
30 Min. 3 mile cross-country run
45 Min. Regular weight workout (Advanced)

Tuesday:

30 Min. Flexibility and warm-up
10 Min. Sprint drills
30 Min. 6 × 330's (90% Anaerobic)

Advanced	Beginners
15 Min. One mile jog—all-out 80 yard finish each lap.	45 Min. Regular weight workout

Wednesday:

30 Min. Flexibility and warm-up
15 Min. 10 × downhill running
20 Min. 2 × 220 at race pace ,
40 Min. 2 × 660 90% of maximum
15 Min. 10 × uphill running
                   Advanced
45 Min. Explosive weight workout

Thursday:

30 Min. Flexibility and warm-up
10 Min. Sprint drills
20 Min. Gun starts
10 Min. 1 × 220 at race pace
30 Min. 6 × Whistlers (relaxation sprinting)

Advanced	Beginners
15 Min. Relay passing	45 Min. Explosive weight workout

Friday:

Rest of optional light loosening workout

Saturday:

Competition

Goal day for beginners on Friday if not running Saturday

Sunday:

Easy relaxed 5 miles on own

SAMPLE WORK WEEK 800—MILE—
TWO MILE (MID-SEASON)

Monday:

30 Min. Flexibility and warm-up
60-70 Min. 10 mile cross-country run
15 Min. 10 × uphill running
45 Min. Regular weight workout (Advanced)

Tuesday:

30 Min. Flexibility and warm-up
15 Min. Pace 220's at race pace
40 Min. 8 × 330's 90% Anaerobic workout

Advanced	Beginners
30 Min. 6 × Whistlers (relaxed sprinting)	45 Min. Regular weight workout

Wednesday:

30 Min. Flexibility and warm-up
15 Min. 10 × downhill running
60 Min. 18 × 440 Interval workout
40 Min. Explosive weight workout (Advanced)

Thursday:.

20 Min. Flexibility and warm-up
15 Min. Pace 220's at race pace

880	Mile and Two Mile
20 Min. 4 × 220's 90% Anaerobic (Adv.)	30 Min. 5 miles cross-country (Adv.)
30 Min. 6 × Whistlers (Advanced)	30 Min. 6 × Whistlers (Advanced)
30 Min. 4 × 220's 90% Anaerobic (Beg.)	30 Min. 5 miles cross-country (Beg.)
15 Min. 3 × Whistlers (Beginners)	15 Min. 3 × Whistlers (Beginners)
45 Min. Explosive weight workout (Beg.)	45 Min. Explosive weight workout (Beg.)

Friday:

Optional rest or light loosening up workout

Saturday:

Competition

Goal day for beginners on Friday if not running Saturday

Sunday:

Easy relaxed 6 miles on own

CHAPTER 6

COACHING THE HURDLE EVENTS

The hurdles represent one of the most fascinating areas of track and field because they encompass elements of both running and field events. Speed and endurance are key factors, but without the development of sound technique, just as in a field event, an athlete is never going to reach maximum potential in the hurdles, regardless of natural ability. Watching a great hurdler in action is one of the great thrills of track and field.

A. SELECTING HURDLERS

Hurdlers need speed, strength, agility, endurance and courage. There are individuals who are the classic hurdler type, tall athletes, especially those who are "split up the middle," blessed with sprinter's speed and flexibility. Don't neglect others, however, who may lack the ideal physical characteristics for the event, but may have a natural instinct for running over barriers. The greatest high hurdler we ever had was only 5'8" and a stocky 165 pounds. This young man became both a Massachusetts and New England champion and, despite his lack of ideal characteristics, had a fantastic instinct for attacking the hurdle, right from the first day he came out for the team.

During our testing process, we run every individual through a hurdles evaluation simply by having them run over a low hurdle several times. The hurdle coach supervises the testing and looks for instinctive lead and trail leg action. Most important of all, however, he looks for

individuals who go right after the hurdle. When selecting hurdle prospects, look for youngsters who do not fear obstacle running and naturally
attack the hurdle. It is very difficult to develop hurdlers out of individuals
who lack this instinct.

You are going to have a lot more success working with the just-
described type of individual at the high school level than you will spend-
ing a lot of time with individuals who may look like hurdlers but lack that
natural attacking instinct. By no means, however, should the athlete with
super hurdling credentials be eliminated if he lacks attacking instinct.
Such an individual is worth the effort needed to develop the necessary
aggressiveness. Only if we find a youngster with the physical credentials
to be a hurdling superstar, do we make this exception, however. No matter how much a youngster looks like a hurdler type, that individual is going to have to overcome timidity toward the barrier if he or she is ever
going to make the grade.

Don't make the mistake of automatically putting your fastest athletes in the sprints and steer the tall ones with decent but not outstanding
speed into the hurdles. There is no question this type of individual may
have a better chance of meeting with success in the hurdles, but the fastest
kid on the team, whom you use in the sprints, may end up just a good one
in that area when he or she could have been a superstar in the hurdles.
Hurdling is a sprint race and the more speed an individual possesses the
better. If you feel a youngster has potential in the hurdles, start that individual off in that area. Our beginning hurdle squad is always much larger
than our beginning sprinters. It is easy to convert a hurdle candidate into
the sprints since they are going to get starting and sprint training anyway.
It is not so easy to make the conversion in the opposite direction.

B. TEACHING HURDLING TECHNIQUE

1. Presenting the event

Presenting the hurdles to prospective candidates should be no different from presenting a field event. We start our beginning hurdlers off with
a classroom presentation to acquaint them with the event just as we do
with a pole vaulter or shot-putter. In such a presentation, begin with loop
films of the greats in action to give the youngsters a feel for the event.
Stress that hurdling is really sprinting over barriers—they are to be run
not jumped over. Emphasize the lay-out action over the hurdle and demonstrate that a great hurdler's head stays at the same level throughout a

race, even when going over the barrier. Emphasize, also, the importance of rhythm, balance and smoothness, as well as the fact that they will be trained to take a definite number of steps to the first and in-between hurdles. Show the loop films over again after making these points. The main thing to accomplish initially is an understanding by the beginner that he or she will be trained in the techniques necessary to sprint over barriers and that hurdling is not a fence-jumping obstacle race.

2. Lead leg action and bar clearance

We believe in teaching hurdling technique over a low hurdle. Once the techniques are reasonably mastered you can move up to the higher barriers. Start the youngsters off by having them walk over the hurdle. Stress a bent lead leg. Tell them to keep the thigh, knee and foot in a straight line and see the knee first and then the foot as they bring the lead leg over the hurdle. At this point do not deal with a correct trail leg action for now; simply tell them to pull it through. (See Figure 6.1.)

In teaching the hurdle clearance position have the candidates assume the familiar hurdle exercise position on the ground. Check them out to be sure they are positioned in three right angles: (1) the angle formed by the inside of the thighs of the lead and trail legs, (2) the angle of the thigh and calf of the trail leg, and (3) the ankle—foot angle of the trail

FIGURE 6.1　Drive into Hurdle

leg. Many youngsters lack the flexibility to get into this position and stay there in good balance. If they cannot assume this position in their own sweet time sitting on the ground, they never are going to do it swiftly in midair clearing a hurdle. This is just one reason why flexibility is so essential in hurdling. We tell our hurdlers to do this hurdle exercise as often as they can and whenever they can, even at home watching TV. This position must become easy and natural.

3. Trail leg action and body angle

Once they have the idea of lead leg action and the proper position over the hurdle bring in the trail leg. Have them stand over the hurdle with the lead leg on the ground as though it had just cleared the barrier. With the trail leg in the just-described right angles, have them bring it through, emphasizing driving the knee up as close to the chest as possible and out to the front. After drilling on the trail leg action alone, have them walk over the hurdle, stressing both lead and trail leg action, emphasizing keeping the shoulders square, the eyes up and the left arm extended slightly forward if the right leg is leading, or the right arm extended forward slightly if the left leg is leading.

After drilling this action walking over the hurdle, have them jog over it, continually increasing speed as their mastery of the technique develops. A gimmick we use with the trail leg action is to tell them to imagine they have two eyes on the inside of the knee of the trail leg and those eyes should be looking at the inside of the other leg as they pull it through. Also, as they start to run over the hurdle rather than walk over it, you should begin to emphasize the forward lean of the body. The amount of lean depends upon the height of the hurdle and the leg split of the athlete. All you want is enough lean so that the trail leg or knee rises like the back end of a seesaw to a level above the hurdle in order for it to be brought through without lifting it. Obviously, this forward lean or dip will vary with individual types and with the height of the hurdle. High hurdlers require more body lean over the hurdle than low hurdlers.(See Figure 6-2.)

4. The takeoff position in relation to the hurdle

The takeoff position is going to vary with the individual. As a standard we set seven feet from the hurdle as the takeoff point, although the ideal spot for some could be a little in either direction. The range should never exceed six–eight feet, however. Emphasize the bent knee

FIGURE 6.2   Forward Lean over Hurdle

lead leg drive and aim the lead heel at a point six inches in front of the hurdle and four inches above it. Stress the downward action of the lead leg from this point, not from directly over or beyond the hurdle. If a beginner shows more than the usual fear of the hurdle, tell that individual to aim a little high. It is far better to have a beginner too high over a hurdle than constantly hitting it. You can always bring a youngster down as he or she progresses. You may never recapture a beginner bruised and discouraged from banging into the barrier.

The location of the takeoff point is one of the most difficult techniques of which you must convince a beginner in any event in track and field. To the beginner, seven and even six feet seem much too far away. There is an extremely natural tendency for the beginner to want to take off much closer to the hurdle. This becomes even a greater factor when you start to teach steps in between hurdles. To get most youngsters to take off from the correct point requires overcoming a major psychological barrier. It is a big selling job and the coach must be aware of it.

5. Timing and landing

The more the athlete progresses with hurdling technique, the more the coach must stress getting down over the hurdle as quickly as possible.

The lead foot should land on the toes about four feet beyond the hurdle, just slightly to the right (if a right lead leg) of an imaginary line down the center of the lane. Once the lead leg begins its downward action, the faster the athlete gets it down, the better. The trail leg must come through very quickly also, but care must be taken not to get over-anxious and begin to bring it through before the ankle clears the crossbar. The athlete should land nearly erect in a good sprinting position. The center of gravity upon landing is directly over the lead leg with the trail knee at the chest on its way through. (See Figure 6-3.)

FIGURE 6.3   Landing Coming off Hurdle

6. Arm action

Arm action is very important, but don't make this a priority in the hurdlers' thinking. The closer you can keep the hurdlers' arm action to that of a sprinter the better. Don't let them exaggerate the extension of the opposite arm to the lead leg. The opposite arm extension should be only sufficient to bring about the necessary lean to get the trail knee higher than the crossbar. Extend it slightly to the inside of the chest line and as it is brought to the rear bring the elbow slightly to the outside so the hand withdraws to the hips as in sprinting action. Be particularly careful not to allow the youngsters to swing the arms laterally. This will rotate the shoulders and cause a loss of balance. Keeping the body in a straight line and in good balnce is an absolute necessity in good hurdling technique.

7. Teaching steps in the boys' high hurdles

As you progress in teaching hurdling technique, raise the bar as soon as you can. It is difficult to learn correct technique over the high barrier and you can easily discourage youngsters. On the other hand, once they begin to get the idea start raising the barrier. You have to start low, but the longer you stay there the greater the psychological adjustment to the highs. Be sure a youngster has developed some confidence in his ability to clear the hurdle properly before you begin to introduce steps.

The standard high hurdling steps are eight to the first barrier and three in between. We have never varied this with any of our high hurdlers. Just because a youngster can get to the first hurdle in seven steps does not mean that is the fastest and most efficient way to get there. I would certainly never force an athlete to use eight steps if he could get the job done better with seven, but I have never had a high school hurdler in 28 years where this would apply. On the other hand, you should force eight rather than nine. Anybody who has to take nine steps to the first hurdle is unlikely to be good enough to make a decent high school hurdling squad. As far as taking more than three steps between hurdles is concerned, the disadvantages are so great it is not even worth consideration.

In teaching steps to the first hurdle it is a good idea to have them run through the eight steps with no barrier at first with you marking where the eighth step lands. Before you introduce the barrier make sure the youngster is confident he can get to the correct take off point in eight steps. Be sure, also, you have sold the youngster on where that take-off point should be.

Once a beginner can get over the first hurdle in the proper steps, we immediately move to three hurdles. We try to get them thinking three steps over three hurdles as soon as possible. It is very important to establish the idea of rhythm in hurdling and this can be accomplished more readily working on three rather than two barriers. If a youngster is running into serious difficulty, it may be necessary to work with just two barriers, but avoid this if you can and the rhythm will come much more readily.

A very common fault in hurdling is maintaining the lean too long. Of course, the less one has to lean to clear the hurdle properly, the better since the goal is always to maintain as close to perfect sprinting form as efficient hurdling technique will allow. High school hurdlers, however, are going to have to lean to some degree and must think—dip and straighten. The timing is very important. As soon as the trail ankle clears the barrier the straightening into good sprinting form begins so that the center of gravity is over the lead leg when it lands. If a youngster is having difficulty with steps, check back for this action. Proper hurdling technique is essential to efficient running of the steps between the hurdles.

Many beginning hurdlers are obsessed with making the steps. There is a great tendency to lean forward in between the hurdles and stretch the stride to make steps. Youngsters who do this have probably not been sold on proper sprinting form in between hurdles and the location of the correct take-off point. One way to deal with this type of youngster is to reduce the distance between the hurdles. It is best if you don't have to do this, but it is a coaching tactic we have often used. It is much more important to teach proper sprinting form between the hurdles and good hurdling technique than it is to make three steps over the correct distance no matter what.

Sometimes it can be effective if you are a bit dishonest in using this tactic. The idea is to shorten the distance between hurdles until a youngster can three-step efficiently and then gradually increase it until he is three-stepping over the regulation distance. Depending on the nature of the individual involved, it might be more effective if he does not realize you are inching the hurdles farther apart and suddenly you present him with the accomplished fact he is three-stepping over the proper distance. If the youngster's problem is psychological and you are confident he has the ability to three-step, then a little trickery here may be the best coaching tactic. If the difficulty in three-stepping is physical, then it is best to keep the process aboveboard. Let him know when you are increasing the distance and only do so when you are confident he can physically handle it.

Again, if you are dealing with a psychological barrier, another coaching tactic is to tell the youngster you are going to move hurdles 2 and 3 two feet closer. The fact is that only the distance between hurdle 1 and 2 is shortened, the distance between 2 and 3 remains the same. It takes a shrewd youngster to figure this out in the middle of a workout. If this works, you once more present the youngster with the accomplished fact that he has three-stepped between hurdles 2 and 3 over the regulation distance. Once again, however, use this only with an individual who is facing a mental barrier. Don't try it if a genuine physical limitation exists.

8. Teaching steps in the girls' hurdles

Since girls run over a low rather than a high hurdle, you do not have the problem of raising the height of the barrier in teaching technique, and should be able to move into steps sooner in the learning process. Although the metric distances to the first hurdle and in between hurdles is slightly shorter than it is for the boys' highs, the step pattern is exactly the same. Championship girl hurdlers use the 8-3 combination just as do boy high hurdlers.

Everything said regarding teaching steps in the highs applies to the girls as well. The main difference is that the girls run over a low hurdle and will not need the same degree of lean over the hurdle as a boy will over the high. In fact, some low hurdlers don't have to lean at all. As said before, the degree of lean over the hurdle depends on the ability of the athlete to get the trail leg high enough to clear the hurdle without having to lift it over the barrier. The degree of lean is strictly an individual matter.

Although the 8-3 combination is a significant goal in the girls' hurdles, the possibility of a 9-4 sequence should not be ruled out for the girls as it should be for the boys. There are two reasons for this: (1) since the girls are running over the low barriers you may well get a small girl with good speed who can master the hurdle technique but just cannnot navigate the 8-3 combination; (2) at the high school level the competition may be such that the type of girl described above using a 9-4 combination could score points and be a productive asset to the team. This is not going to be true with the boys but it can be with the girls. If you have the type of girl just described and she can master the alternating technique that requires being able to lead with either leg you should give the 9-4 combination some consideration.

As a girl moves up in class the validity of this alternative decreases proportionately. No one is going to four-step successfully against real championship competition. Never use a 9-4 concept as a crutch or expedient for a girl with significant potential. Girls' track is progressing fantastically and the day may come when the 9-4 combination is just as invalid for the girls as it is for the boys (possibly in your area that day has arrived already). In most cases, however, at the high school level of girls' track there still may be a place for the talented little four-stepper.

9. Teaching steps in the boys' 330 intermediate and low hurdles

Some states run the 330 hurdles over the intermediate hurdle as do the colleges, while others, like Massachusetts, run the 330's over the conventional low hurdle. If the former is the case in your state, then more time must be spent on technique and raising the barrier in the learning process. Also, if you are using the intermediates you may not be able to get away with utilizing certain sprint types in this event as we do in Massachusetts. It takes a better hurdler to run the 330 intermediates than it does to run the 330 lows. Acknowledging this fact, the problems in dealing with these events are still essentially the same.

There is no question that there is an advantage in leading with the left leg running the intermediate hurdles because some of the hurdles must be taken on the curve. It would be a mistake, however, to insist a youngster lead with the left leg if that is going to interrupt rhythm and smoothness. The advantage of the left lead leg on the curve definitely does not offset a loss of rhythm. It is far better to have a smooth, efficient hurdler leading with the right leg on a curve than an awkward one leading with the left.

There is no definite number of steps to the first hurdle or in between hurdles in the intermediate that applies to everyone. Steps are an individual matter. What may be ideal for some will be a strain for others. The key is rhythm and smoothness. What is important is not how few steps one can take, but the efficiency of their execution and the overall time of the race. The average high school hurdler will probably take 21 steps to the first hurdle and 17 in between, but there are great numbers who successfully utilize some other combination. You must work individually with each athlete and determine what is best for him.

It is absolutely necessary to have a step sequence in intermediate hurdling, and, in arriving at that sequence, there are two critical decisions you may be forced to make. (1) The first decision involves the possibility of running an even rather than an odd number of steps. Some world class hurdlers run 13 steps between hurdles, while others compete very successfully with 15. Although some top-notchers at the high school level can handle 15, 17 is much more likely for the average youngster. An odd number is best because it provides for the same lead leg action over each hurdle. For some, however, 15 is just too few and 17 is going to cause severe chopping. If we discount technique over the hurdle and consider only smoothness, rhythm and efficiency of the run, 16 may be ideal for many youngsters. For these individuals the question is, should he run over the hurdles with good action but chop steps, or should he run smoothly between the hurdles with the disadvantage of alternating lead legs? The answer lies in what disrupts him the most. If an athlete can learn to master leading with either leg reasonably well and the even number of steps leads to definite efficiency of the run, then I believe strongly that he ought to alternate. Such a situation is more likely to be the case if your state runs the 330 lows rather than the intermediate height hurdles. If alternating lead legs disrupts him more than taking the extra step, however, then take the extra step. You must make the judgment upon the overall efficiency of performance of the entire event.

(2) The second critical decision involves whether or not to change the number of steps between the hurdles in the middle of the race. Many great ones have run the first part of the race in 13 steps and then switched over to 15 and have done so very successfully. Some at the high school level will go from 15 to 17. Such an action does involve a drastic alteration of stride. Again the key is how much such a move disrupts smoothness and rhythm. If you are assessing such a tactic, be sure you judge it upon the efficiency of the entire 330 yards and not upon the speed with which the first few hurdles are run with the lesser number of steps. A severe slowing down in the latter stages of a race may mistakenly be blamed upon a youngster's conditioning when the real culprit may be the strain imposed upon him by running the first few hurdles with too few steps. If an athlete cannot run the entire race with the same number of steps between hurdles, there is a a problem somewhere. Be sure you are certain that changing steps in the middle of a race is the most efficient way to run the entire race before you adopt this tactic. It may well be, but be sure.

It would appear that switching from say 15 to 16 steps in between hurdles in the middle of a race would result in two alterations, number of steps and lead legs, and this would be extremely disruptive to rhythm. Although this could possibly be the most efficient combination for some individuals, I would be particularly hesitant in adopting it.

Whatever you do, don't force an intermediate hurdler into a step combination with which he is not comfortable and confident. This is by far the most important factor in this event. Most intermediate hurdle races are lost at the high school level because a youngster begins to lose confidence and starts chopping steps. My experience has been that step breakdown is the chief fault in the intermediate hurdles at the high school level. Most often, also, it is a psychological rather than a physical phenomenon.

Chopping usually begins three or four strides before take off and there is no way for a hurdler to be sure his steps are off at that point. He just thinks they are off. The coach must do a real selling job to establish confidence so the athlete will carry through the step combination decided upon, no matter what.

10. The start

As far as starting is concerned, there is no difference between the hurdle and sprint starts. The same teaching methods and techniques are utilized as were explained in the chapter on sprinting. The only difference is that boys in the high hurdles and girl hurdlers must come up into the full sprinting stride less gradually than a sprinter would. The distance to the first hurdle in the high is 15 yards and for the girls slightly less than that. In order to get proper drive into the take-off the hurdler ought to be in full sprinting stride at least two strides before the take-off. In view of this, a high or girl hurdler should still come out of the blocks low, just like a sprinter, but should come up into sprinter's stride a little quicker and less gradually. In the intermediate hurdles this problem does not exist.

Since most hurdlers run eight steps to the first hurdle, this may present the question, should the lead leg be changed so that the hurdler uses the most natural foot placement in the blocks or should the block placement be changed? Of course, if an athlete leads with the left leg and also starts with the left leg back in the blocks, or vice versa, there is no problem. Often, however, this is not the case. If you are faced with this decision, leave the lead leg alone and change the block positioning. It has been my experience that changing the back and forward feet in the blocks is not as disruptive as changing the lead leg over the hurdle.

The above could be a factor in determining the number of steps to the first hurdle in the intermediates. If an athlete leads over the hurdle naturally with the left leg and also starts most naturally with the left leg back in the blocks then an even number of steps to the first hurdle might be best. If the athlete naturally leads with the left leg, but prefers the right leg back in the blocks, the use of an odd number of steps to the first hurdle might be best. In my judgment, however, the most efficient number of steps to the first hurdle is the most vital factor. I would not fool with this nor would I alter the natural lead leg. If an alteration is necessary, then change the foot positioning in the blocks.

11. Dealing with the problem of hitting hurdles

Banging into the hurdle can not only become a serious physical problem, but it can develop a serious psychological barrier in the event as well. No matter how little fear of the hurdle a youngster may have, he or she can still get bruised and broken, and fear will eventually creep in. This is a major reason for beginning your teaching over the low hurdle. Padding the crossbars with foam rubber in practice can also be an effective tactic. If the youngster is hitting the lead leg, it is probably either the result of bringing the lead leg up straight rather than with a good bent leg leading with the knee, or it can be the result of taking off too close or too far away from the hurdle.

If the trail leg is hitting the hurdle, it is the result of not getting proper lean. Here one encounters a serious psychological problem. When a beginner thinks he or she is going to hit a hurdle, the natural tendency is to lift quickly with the head and trunk. Psychologically this is natural but you want just the opposite reaction. To get the trail leg up, you must bring the head and trunk down, in other words, lean. To help them understand this, use the analogy of a seesaw. When one end goes up, the other end goes down. Until beginners understand this principle and react properly to it, they will get some pretty good bumps just reacting naturally.

12. Poise

The most important ingredient a hurdler can possess is poise. There is a great tendency to strain and lose form when a race gets competitive in the late stages. Hurdlers must be constantly reminded of the importance of relaxation and warned that they must keep their poise at all costs. They must understand that if someone is faster at the end of a race, then they are just faster. Straining at the bit and losing poise is not going to remedy the situation. All runners have to face this problem, but on the flat it only results in losing, over the hurdles it can mean crashing into the barrier and disaster. Losing poise is an improper reaction to challenge. Keep this problem in the open and discuss it frequently with your hurdlers. Never take the question of poise for granted. The chances of an individual's losing poise in a challenging situation are decreased considerably if he or she has been psychologically prepared for it.

C. TRAINING BOY HIGH HURDLERS

Essentially high hurdlers should be trained as sprinters doing double duty in the 100 and 220. They need both the sheer speed of the former and the staying power of the latter. Running 120 yards over 39" barriers is not the same as running 120 yards on the flat. High hurdlers should do all the same basic work as do sprinters. We emphasize downhill running, uphill running, relaxation sprinting or "Whistlers", starting work and anaerobic repeat work. A top-flight high hurdler should be able to run a strong 220.

A high hurdler must do a great deal of work over the hurdles to develop technique and confidence, but you cannot do the same amount of work running over barriers as you can with flat running. For this reason we like to do at least half of our running workouts on the flat. Hurdling is a technique event, just like the field events. In track and field you should not work technique when an athlete is getting tired as the effort expended will soon become counter-productive. Numerous times in this book the coaching error of attempting to accomplish two things at once will be stressed. This is particularly true of hurdling. Concentrate on technique work in the first half of the practice session when the youngsters are still fresh; do the heavy flat running portion afterward.

It is not necessary, nor is it good practice, to run a lot of full-flight hurdles. A well conditioned hurdler with excellent technique over five hurdles is not going to have difficulty with ten. When running the full flight use the same rule as in any time trial or in going all-out in a field event. Running the full flight should be regarded as competition. Be sure the athletes are well rested and psychologically prepared for it. An unsuccessful full flight of hurdling can do a great deal of damage psychologically to a youngster's confidence.

Timing is of the essence in hurdling. Except when teaching the techniques or in certain drills, never go over hurdles in training unless it is all-out. It is extremely easy to develop bad habits and to get injured if timing is thrown off. Taking it easy in trial heats of the hurdles is equally dangerous. If you have an individual that superior to the competition, ease him off after clearing the final barrier—don't invite disaster.

D. TRAINING GIRL HURDLERS

Since the girls run about 10 yards less than the boys and run over the low rather than the high hurdles, technique and staying power are not as great problems. Everything is relative, however, and I see no good reason to train girls in the 100-meter low hurdles any differently than boys are trained for the highs. The amount of time devoted to technique in any training program for hurdlers depends upon the particular weaknesses in technique of each individual. In my judgment, if you made a comparison of a top-flight female and a male hurdler, each ideally suited for their event, the girl hurdler would not find her event as demanding physically as would her male counterpart in the highs. As a result, a class girl hurdler should be able to spend more time on sheer sprinting work to develop greater speed. Most of our girls, however, are not class athletes and find their hurdling event just as demanding as do the boys, and are trained accordingly. Needless to say, excess baggage is a real problem for the hurdlers and proper dieting habits are essential here as well as in all running and jumping events.

E. TRAINING BOY INTERMEDIATE HURDLERS

Without question, the 330 intermediates, or lows for that matter, are as demanding an event as there is in track and field. Essentially, competitors in this event should be trained as quarter milers. In addition to basic sprinting work, the intermediate hurdler must get a heavy does of repeat anaerobic work and over-distance work. An athlete must be in superb physical condition and know it in order to have the confidence necessary to maintain steps, rhythm and good technique throughout the distance.

If an athlete can run a solid quarter mile, he can run a strong 330 over the hurdles. If your intermediate hurdlers are good enough to double in the mile relay, there are great physical and psychological advantages in so doing. The intermediate hurdler must be trained to cope with oxygen debt and quarter-mile training is the area where that is given the most extensive attention.

The same policies regarding work over the hurdles and flat running aply to the intermediates just as in the highs. The wisdom of never running the full distance over the hurdles unless physically rested and psychologically prepared is probably never more valid than in this event. Unsuccessful full run-throughs are the last thing in the world you want in the 330's. All training for the intermediates must be geared to relaxation, poise and confidence.

F. FLEXIBILITY AND STRENGTH

It is virtually impossible to master proper hurdling technique without a substantial degree of flexibility in the athlete. In addition to the standard flexibility exercises done by the entire team at the beginning of practice, hurdlers should include in their practice sessions all the standard hurdling exercises with which all coaches are familiar. Hurdlers, in fact, should be encouraged to go through all their flexibility and hurdling exercises as well as during the regular practice sessions.

Strength is also vital to good hurdling as it is to all events in track and field. Our hurdlers are encouraged to work on a year-round program lifting three times a week in the off-season and twice a week while competing. They work on the same program as our sprinters and quarter milers. Strength and flexibility are absolute essentials to hurdling success.

SAMPLE WORK WEEK BOYS' HIGH HURDLES AND GIRLS' HURDLES

Monday:

30 Min. Flexibility and warm-up
10 Min. Additional hurdle stretching
40 Min. Technique work over hurdles
30 Min. 4 × 330's 90% Anaerobic workout
15 Min. 10 × uphill running
45 Min. Regular weight workout
       (Advanced)

Tuesday:

30 Min. Flexibility and warm-up
10 Min. Additional hurdle stretching
15 Min. Gun starts over one hurdle
20 Min. 3 competitive runs over 5 hurdles
15 Min. 10 × downhill running

Advanced	Beginners
15 Min. 10 × uphill running	45 Min. Regular weight workout

Wednesday:

30 Min. Flexibility and warm-up
10 Min. Additional hurdle stretching
40 Min. 4 × 120's (girls' 100 meter)
       over first 5 flights remainder
       over flat concentrating on relaxed
       finish
15 Min. Weight jacket running
30 Min. 6 × Whistlers (relaxation
       sprinting)
10 Min. 550 Yard run (90%)
45 Min. Explosive weight workout
       (Advanced)

Thursday:

30 Min. Flexibility and warm-up
10 Min. Additional hurdle stretching
20 Min. Technique work over hurdles

SAMPLE WORK WEEK
BOYS' HIGH HURDLES AND GIRLS' HURDLES (*cont.*)

Thursday: (*Continued*)

20 Min. 4 gun starts over 2 hurdles
15 Min. 10 × downhill running

Advanced	Beginners
30 Min. 4 × 330's slow-fast (1/2 at 80% 1/2 all out relaxed)	15 Min. 2 × 330's slow-fast 45 Min. Explosive weight workout

Friday:

Rest or optional light loosening workout

Saturday:

Goal day for beginners on Friday if not running Saturday

Sunday:

Easy relaxed 3 miles on own

SAMPLE WORK WEEK 330 LOW OR INTERMEDIATE HURDLES

Monday:

30 Min. Flexibility and warm-up
10 Min. Additional stretching for hurdles
20 Min. Hurdle technique work over low
(Intermediate) hurdles at high
hurdle spacing
20 Min. 4 competitive starts over first
hurdle
30 Min. Ladder anaerobic workout
45 Min. Regular weight workout
(Advanced)

Tuesday:

30 Min. Flexibility and warm-up
10 Min. Additional hurdle stretching
40 Min. 3 × 330's over the first 4 flights,
remainder over flat concentrating
on a relaxed finish
15 Min. 10 × downhill running
15 Min. 10 × uphill running

Advanced	Beginners
20 Min. 3 miles cross-country run	45 Min. Regular weight workout

Wednesday:

30 Min. Flexibility and warm-up
15 Min. Hurdle technique work over low
        (intermediate) hurdle at high
        hurdle spacing
25 Min. 3 runs over first 3 hurdles
        concentrating on steps
40 Min. 3 × 660's at 80%
45 Min. Explosive weight workout
        (Advanced)

Thursday:

30 Min. Flexibility and warm-up
10 Min. Additional hurdle stretching
20 Min. Hurdle technique work over low
        (intermediate) hurdle at high
        hurdle spacing
20 Min. Competitive starts over first
        hurdle
30 Min. 4 × 330's slow fast (1/2 80%
        1/2 all out relaxed)

Advanced	Beginners
15 Min. 1 × 550 at 90%	45 Min. Explosive weight workout

Friday:

Optional rest or light loosening workout

Saturday:

Competition
Goal day for beginners on Friday if not running Saturday

Sunday:

Easy relaxed 5 miles on own

CHAPTER 7

COACHING THE HIGH JUMP

A. PRESENTING THE EVENT

Like just about everybody else, we have made a full commitment to the Flop style of jumping. The Straddle is an efficient method of jumping and some great ones still use it. When the Flop first came out we attempted to assess each individual and determine what style was best suited for each athlete. This didn't work very well and, with the time limitations we all face at the high school level, it actually became counterproductive. It became very obvious that beginners were able to attain respectable heights much more readily with the Flop than the Straddle. The Flop enables the jumper to more easily convert speed into vertical lift and there is much less of a tendency to begin the roll over the bar before completing the vertical lift, a major problem with the Straddle for beginners.

In the initial classroom session with prospective high jumpers considerable time should be spent with loop films in order to give beginners a picture of what the Flop looks like. As with all field events, the high jump should be presented as a sequence event, with each stage being completed before the next stage begins. In the high jump there are three basic stages; the run up or approach, the take-off or vertical lift, and the bar clearance. It is vital for beginners to understand that these three stages must blend together into one smooth action, but that serious problems are caused when there is an attempt to rush things and overlap them.

121

It is also important that beginners initially understand the need for rotation during the vertical lift so that the body will pass over the bar perpendicular to it. They must understand that the curved approach into the take-off makes this rotation possible. Also, the basic fundamental that one must gain complete vertical lift first and clear the bar afterward should be carefully explained. We want every beginner to be fully aware that the most basic fault of new high jump prospects is a desire to be overanxious in getting the body over the bar, resulting in a loss of vertical lift. To prove this point, we take the jumping prospects into the gym immediately upon finishing the classroom presentation and stand them under the basketball baskets. We then tell them to lean over backward in the position a flopper would be in when clearing the bar, and, without raising the trunk, jump up and touch the basket. Needless to say, they are lucky to get off the ground from this position. At this point we tell them to jump up and touch the rim in their own way. Everybody will now jump into the air with their trunks directly over their take-off legs. Just about everybody has some basketball experience and this is an illustration they can readily understand. Before we ever start to teach the techniques of high jumping on the field, we want to impress as strongly as possible just how much one loses in vertical lift by attempting to roll over the bar too soon.

B. TEACHING THE HIGH JUMP

1. The Run-up

The vertical lift demonstration in the gym, just described, also serves a second purpose. It enables the coach to determine the natural jumping foot, or take-off leg, of each prospect. Once this determination is made, we start our prospective floppers off by teaching them to run in a circle. Spread all the jumpers into two circles about 15 yards in diameter each. All the jumpers in one of the circles will be the left-foot jumpers and they will run counterclockwise. Those that take off on the right leg will be in the second circle and they will run clockwise. In both circles, the young athletes will get the feel of leaning in and runnning at the same time with the inside arm swinging in a shorter arc than the outside. This should be followed up by having them come in on a curved run and jumping up to touch the basket rim. It is important at this stage to have them get the idea of obtaining vertical lift from a curved run-up.

2.The double armed lift

One of the most difficult aspects of flop jumping is the timing of the double-arm lift action with the knee lift of the lead leg. This action should be taught in a straight line before adapting it to the curved run-up. Have the jumpers stand in a running position with the left leg forward, the right arm forward and the left arm back (for jumpers who take off on the left foot). Jumpers who take off on the right foot should stand with the right leg and left arm forward, and the right arm back. At this point the process will be described for the individual who takes off on the left foot.

Walk the youngsters through the process in this manner. (1) Holding the right arm in the forward position, step forward with the right leg bringing the left arm forward with it so it catches up with the right arm. (2) Bring the left leg forward and swing both arms together in a backward arc causing a natural settling of the body. The athlete has now completed the last two steps in the run-up. (3) Bring the right knee up high, as in the take-off action, bringing both arms up in a driving action synchronized with the right knee lift. We have now completed a simulation of the last two strides of the run-up and the take-off action.

Once they have mastered the above sequence, have the athletes walk through a 10-step approach, still in a straight line, repeating the above action on the last two strides. When they can handle the action from a 10-step walk-up, have them repeat the process from a very slow jog. Gradually increase the speed of the run until the athlete has mastered the action at roughly the speed you wish to employ in actual jumping. (See Figure 7.1.)

FIGURE 7.1 Double Arm Lift

3. Introducing the curved run and the takeoff

Once the double arm action is synchronized in a straight line run, the athlete is ready to learn the takeoff running in from a curve. At this point, still do not introduce measured steps. Ask each jumper to come into the bar in a curve with the bar set at a height the jumper can easily handle. Stress a slight shortening of the final step and a foot placement of the takeoff leg parallel to the bar. Have them drive the right or lead knee across the body as close to the head as possible. We like to tell the youngsters to "pop the head off the body". Don't complicate the process by mentioning a lean-back position of the body as a proper double arm action should lend itself to an adequate settling. Further, you want as explosive an action on the vertical lift as possible and should not hinder it with any unnecessary thinking at this point. You can always work on this later if you are not satisfied with the backward lean.

A major factor in a good takeoff is the full extension of the left or take-off ankle. Hopefully you can get this without forcing the athlete to think about it. If you can't, then you must emphasize the point because it is so important. If the action is performed correctly, a definite rotation should be taking place during the takeoff and should be completed with the jumper's back to the bar by the time the athlete leaves the ground. Again, if you can accompish this without forcing the athlete to think about it, you are that much ahead of the game. What should be stressed here is keeping everything tight with a perpendicular position at take-off so that all force is in a vertical direction.

4. Bar clearance

Once a decent vertical lift and rotation have been established, begin to raise the bar slightly and emphasize clearance. Up to this point let nature take its course. When you are ready to teach clearance, an important coaching point at this stage is to stress bringing the take-off leg up to join the lead leg. Beginners often bring the lead leg down and end up sitting on the bar. The position of the arms at this point is also vital. Mediocre jumpers tend to throw their right arms into the pit and defeat the purpose of the "J" run. Stress hands on the thighs and arms to the side during the action over the bar. The body should pass over the bar perpendicular to it. Tell the jumper to look over the right shoulder bringing the chin to the chest. We like to tell them, "try to look at your spine." To do this, the jumper must keep the back arched and the hips up. Spreading the knees at this point also helps this action considerably. Tell the jumper to hold the arch in the back as long as he or she can. (See Figure 7.2.)

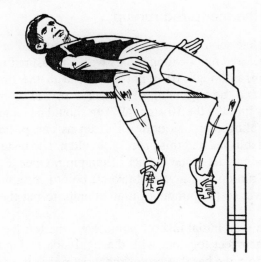

FIGURE 7.2   Position over Bar

Critical to the success of the flop jump is the timing of the next action. As soon as the jumper's hips clear the bar, he should pike. Tell him to turn the head up and look at the knees. This should result in losing the arch of the back and the lowering of the hips so the legs can be flipped over the bar. The jumper cannot see where he or she is and has to develop a critical sense of timing. You, as the coach, can aid the jumper in developing this sense of timing by hollering "Up" at the right moment. You can simulate and drill on this action by having the athlete lay on his or her back on the jumping pit with the legs bent over the side. From this position have the athlete turn the chin to the chest, arch the back and raise the hips—hold it in that position—then look up at the knees as the legs are flipped up. (See Figure 7.3.)

FIGURE 7.3   Leg Clearance

5. Adding the measured run-up

The athlete should have the previously described process reasonably well down before complicating things with a measured run-up. We teach a 10-step run, although 10 is not sacred, with the first six steps in a straight line and the beginning of the curve or "J" commencing on the seventh step. Initially the 10-step "J" run should be taught away from the jumping pit altogether. As uniform a run as can possibly be obtained should be established and this process should not be disturbed by even the presence of a bar, let alone the act of jumping. Once a smooth, uniform 10-step "J" run up to a mythical takeoff point is established, then bring the athlete over to the jumping pit an attempt to put the whole business together.

To obtain an initial takeoff point, have the left leg takeoff jumpers stand with their feet together with the right side facing the bar at a distance away from the bar that brings the wrist right over the bar. The position of the left foot is now the distance it should be out from the bar at takeoff. In addition, the takeoff spot should be located 18″ inside the near standard. This is, of course, only a beginning position as the takeoff point for each individual has to be adjusted so that maximum height is directly over the bar. The above system has worked well for us, however, as a starter.

C. TRAINING THE HIGH SCHOOL HIGH JUMPER

1. Technique training

We like to keep the bar low for high jumpers during the learning process. Once the basics have been taught, however, and you are into the competitive season, there is little value in practicing at low heights unless there is the need to correct some flagrant flaw that has developed. Our standard practice sessions involve jumping for technique at four inches below the best height achieved by a particular jumper. It is important, however, not to be locked into any one practice height. If an athlete continually fails at the four inches below maximum height suggested, drop it down. If failure continues even after dropping the height, stop jumping altogether. There is only so much spring in an athlete's legs on any given day. If the spring isn't there and the youngster shows definite signs of fatigue, don't force him or her to continue jumping. Technique work can be extremely counter-productive when the spring is lacking and is accompanied by repeated failure.

Some individuals may learn lessons from failure, but it is extremely difficult to alter technique in a positive direction through failure. High jumpers, like pole vaulters, are constantly faced with the psychological phenomenon of failure. A shot putter makes a poor throw—it simply doesn't go very far, it doesn't get measured and who cares. Long and triple jumpers usually react to a poor jump in the same manner. When a high jumper makes a poor jump the bar is knocked down and there is a very direct psychological message of failure. There is clearly a different image planted in the high jumper's mind. Guard against this. It is vitally important in the coaching process to keep failure down to a minimum.

A particularly serious error in high jumping is to continually raise the height of the bar during practice sessions, concluding a workout with jumping at high heights. Just when the athlete needs it the most, the physical ability to perform the event is diminishing rapidly or is disappearing altogether. If you are planning to jump for height, be sure the jumper is both mentally and physically prepared to do so. You would never send a tired athlete into actual jumping competition, so don't ask the youngster to go for height in practice unless you have given that individual the same type of preparation you would for a meet. All you will accomplish if you do not heed this rule is failure, compounded by the fact you have weakened that particular youngster's confidence in his or her ability to make that particular height. A jumper who lacks the confidence to make a certain height has very little chance of ever making it. It is much like the baseball player who goes up to bat expecting to strike out—he usually does.

i. Preparation for competition

It is very important to prepare a jumper psychologically for heights he or she has never made before. The best way not to do it is by establishing a long record of failure in practice. It is necessary to give the youngster something to grab on to in competition, and an understanding of adrenalin can be the secret. Convince the jumper that he or she will have something working in competition that just is never there in a practice situation. As the adrenalin starts pumping, the spring is going to increase. As coaches we all know this. The important thing is to convince the athlete. It is essential to convince the youngster that when a height never achieved before is reached, nothing should be done differently to get over the bar. There is a tremendous tendency among high jumpers to try too hard and destroy technique when jumping at a previously unattained height. How often have we all seen an athlete having a good day jump up to a previous best then completely fall apart when a new maximum is attempted. The reason is inevitably that the jumper was not psychologically prepared in advance for this situation. When the confidence is lacking he will consciously or unconsciously resort to something different in a futile effort to make the height.

Make your athletes aware of the boost adrenalin can give them and the folly of doing anything that will disrupt their technique. Every high jumper should go into competition with complete confidence that he or she can make heights never achieved before because of the adrenalin factor as long as there is no falling off in technique. Do everything you can also to convince the youngster that you have complete confidence in his or her ability to make the new height in question. Your confidence has a way of rubbing off on an athlete, just as does your lack of confidence. If you can sell the youngster on his or her ability to make a height, that individual will give it his or her best shot. The athlete may still not make it, but without that best shot, there really isn't any chance. Falling apart at previously unattained heights is the product of never really giving the matter prior thought and the failure of the coach to provide the proper positive guidance in meeting the challenge.

ii. When to stop jumping

Another unique feature of high jumping and pole vaulting not present in other track and field events is that competition invariably ends in failure. Even the winner of the event keeps going until he or she misses. It is not always the wisest procedure for the winner of an event to keep on jumping. You, as the coach, should carefully analyze the situation when a jumper has eliminated all the competition. What is the individual's emotional state? How many jumps have already been taken? How tired does the youngster appear to be? Are you going to ask that individual to play a further significant role in the meet? All of these factors should influence your decision as to whether or not the youngster should keep on jumping. If in your judgement the athlete is in the right frame of mind and has a good chance of going higher, then by all means encourage him or her to go on. Never throw away the opportunity to climb another psychological plateau. On the other hand, if you have a gut feeling the youngster has peaked for the day, you should seriously consider stopping at that point. There is nothing in the rules that says an athlete must keep on jumping until he or she misses. If the youngster is on a real emotional high after winning and making a particular height, it may be good judgment to let the individual go home on "Cloud 9" rather than with another experience in failing at a new height, an experience that may weaken confidence and destroy that great emotional lift. The wise coach knows when to keep going and when to turn the engine off and save it for another day.

2. Strength training

In the off-season and the early regular season all high jumpers work on a three-session-per-week schedule utilizing the regular workout concept described in Chapter 2. As soon as the competitive season begins we cut back to a twice weekly regular-explosive sequence. Whenever possible on alternate days we do three sets of 10 on the Leaper Machine as well as weight jacket work, but take great care never to do any work of this type the day before any competitive jumping and two days prior to a major meet or serious challenge. With high jumpers, the greatest emphasis should be upon the leg work but exercises for the abdomen, lower back and upper body should not be neglected.

Free Weight Workout:	Weight Machine Workout:
Heel Raises	Heel Raises (Free weights)
Squats	Squats (Free weights)
Leg Extensions (Machine)	Leg Extensions
Leg Curls (Machine)	Leg Curls
Inclined sit-ups	Inclined sit-ups
Leg Lifts	Leg lifts
Bench press	Dips
Military press	Front Trunk twists
Forearm curls	Bench press
Upright rowing	Military press
	Forearm curls
	Upright rowing
	Kneeling pulldowns

3. Running workouts

All of our high jumpers do a great deal of running with the sprinters or hurdlers. Many of them participate in these events also. We insist on a good running workout in every practice session under normal conditions. Great care should be taken with those individuals who are primarily high jumpers, however. The high jump coach handles every phase of their training. If a runner also high jumps for points, the running coach handles that individual's running workouts, but never if the high jump is a particular athlete's main event. More than any other event, in my judgment, high jumpers can be adversely effected by 50-50 training with some other event. Athletes whose prime contribution to the team is high jumping train as high jumpers, and if the individual is a decent runner, he or she will compete in the running event for points for the team. High jumping and hurdling is a common double in high school track and field and it is no coincidence that I have always assigned the same coach to both areas. If they are better as jumpers, train them as jumpers and let them run for gravy points. If they are better as runners, train them as runners and let them jump for gravy points. Never go 50-50 with a high jumper.

D. ANALYZING THE MOST COMMON FAULTS IN HIGH SCHOOL JUMPERS

1. Coming in too straight to the bar

i. Cause

This is a matter of not concentrating on the run-up to the bar. If the athlete loses the curve approach to the bar, he or she will end up with the take-off foot pointing at the bar instead of parallel to it. This greatly impairs rotation and results in the jumper's passing over the bar at an excessive angle to it rather than perpendicular.

ii. Correction

If the athlete is not concentrating on the run, the best cure is to get that individual away from the jumping pit and go back to working on the "J" approach without the distraction of the pit and the jumping process. It is always advantageous to isolate a fault in the correcting process. In most cases this cannot be done, but it is possible in dealing with the run-up in high jumping.

2. Failure to get maximum height directly over the bar

i. Cause

This extremely common fault is caused by a flaw in the run-up, resulting in the athlete's being either too close or too far away from the bar at take-off.

ii. Correction

The importance of a good uniform run cannot be over-emphasized. Even with a good uniform run, however, obtaining maximum height in the wrong place happens with the best of them. It is more difficult to run exactly the same way every time on a curve than it is in a straight line. You must not only keep the speed and length of stride consistent, but the degree of the curve as well. If this occurs in practice you simply go back to emphasizing the "J" run-up, away from the pit if the problem becomes serious enough. If the fault develops during competition, however, as it often does, it is a different matter.

An extremely difficult decision a coach and jumper must make during competition is whether or not to adjust the starting mark up or back depending on whether maximum height is being gained in front of or behind the bar. The key to this decision lies in analyzing the run-up for smoothness and consistency. If the athlete has good rhythm and is not losing his or her uniform run, yet is still gaining maximum height in the wrong place as a result of taking off too close or too far away from the bar, then it is likely that conditions of the approach surface, weather, etc. are affecting the location of the take-off point. If this is the case the coach should recommend a slight adjustment in the starting mark. If, however, there does not appear to be good rhythm in the run-up, the jumper is a bit rattled and changing marks may only lead to further confusion. If an athlete has lost the uniform run, hitting the take-off mark properly becomes a matter of chance and the odds are better to hit the take-off point correctly sticking to what the individual is used to rather than fooling around with the starting mark in the middle of competition.

The point here is that you should not automatically and arbitrarily make adjustments in an athlete's marks during competition. Obviously, a proper adjustment can be the difference between success and failure and when called for such an adjustment must be made. The key is to make such a move only when a consistent pattern has developed and only when it has been determined that outside forces are responsible for the incorrect take-off point.

3. Attempting to clear bar before completing vertical lift

i. Cause

This problem is almost always the result of over-anxiousness and can be identified by the athlete's throwing the inside hand into the pit. Since the goal of high jumping is to get over the bar, the less poised individual is going to attempt to do so as quickly as possible.

ii. Correction

We like to tell our jumpers, "Your brains are in your head and they want to get over the bar first. Tell your brains to be patient." Patience and emphasis upon proper timing and execution of the double arm action and vertical lift are the keys here. Go back to your take-off drills if this problem is developing. Equally important, however, is the recognition by the jumper that this is a tendency all high jumpers must guard against. This is why we put such great emphasis upon this point in the initial class room presentation, and we never let up reminding the athletes to be patient and not rush getting over the bar.

4. Hitting the bar with the hips or legs

i. Cause

Assuming everything prior to bar clearance has been done correctly, this problem is caused by improper timing of the hip and leg clearnace.

ii. Correction

A key factor in dealing with improper hip and leg clearance is the location of the head. The chin should be on the chest during hip clearance and looking up at the knees during the leg flip. We do a lot of drilling on this, lying in the pit as previously described in order to make the process a completely habitual action. As was said earlier, this timing is also a matter of instinct and the coach's hollering "Up" at just the right time in practice can be helpful in developing the proper sense of timing. Watch out, however, not to continue doing this once the athlete gets the hang of it. Don't become a crutch for the jumper and create a dependence upon your call.

E. SPECIAL PROBLEMS IN COACHING
GIRL HIGH JUMPERS

There is absolutely no difference in technique for girl high jumpers nor are there any differences in training methods. The only difference between the boys and girls may be in leg strength in some cases. This is, of course, relative as most girls do not have as much body mass to drive up in the air as their male counterparts. There is a chance, however, that some of your girls may begin to lose the spring in the legs quicker on a given day than athletes with greater leg strength. As previously stated, it is unwise to keep jumping an athlete when the spring in the legs begins to diminish seriously. You should be a little more conscious of dealing with this with the girls.

In all events in girls' track and field, with the exception of the throws, weight and body development is a major problem. There is no event where this shows up more readily than in the high jump. Maintaining proper habits of diet is important to all athletes and girl high jumpers in particular. You cannot control nature and certain girls are going to develop in ways that may be attractive to the figure but are disadvantageous to high jumping no matter how careful that individual is with her dieting habits. You can control weight, however, and that must be a major priority for all girl jumpers and runners. All high jumpers should do a lot of running and in the case of girls with a weight problem, a lot of long, slow distance running which burns off the calories is advisable. No matter what you do, you are going to experience the trauma of seeing outstanding girl high jumping prospects go over the hill midway through high school because of body development. With good dieting and training programs, however, you can at least slow the process down. This is a major reason why it is vital to get girl high jumpers started as early as possible.

SAMPLE HIGH JUMP WORK WEEK (MID-SEASON)

Monday:

30 Min. Flexibility and warm-up
10 Min. Additional stretching and warm-up jumping
30 Min. Technique jumping at non-challenging height
30 Min. 4 × 220's 90%
45 Min. Regular weight workout (Advanced)
       Rope skipping and leaper machine (Beginners)

Tuesday:

30 Min. Flexibility and warm-up
15 Min. Circle running drill
15 Min. Circle running drill jumping at overhead object
20 Min. Hurdling for rhythm
15 Min. 10 × downhill running
15 Min. 6 × 110's 80% walking in between
45 Min. Rope skipping and leaper machine (Advanced)
       Regular weight workout (Beginners)

Wednesday:

30 Min. Flexibility and warm-up
10 Min. Additional stretching and warm-up jumping
45 Min. Technique jumping at near maximum height
30 Min. 3 × 440's 90%
45 Min. Explosive weight workout (Advanced)
       Rope skipping and leaper machine (Beginners)

Thursday:

30 Min. Flexibility and warm-up
15 Min. Check out steps
15 Min. Hurdling for rhythm
30 Min. 6 × Whistlers (relaxation sprinting)
20 Min. Easy 2 1/2 mile cross-country run
45 Min. Rope skipping and leaper machine (Advanced)
　　　　　Explosive weight workout (Beginners)

Friday:

Rest or optional light loosening workout (Advanced)

Goal Day (Beginners)

Saturday:

Competition

CHAPTER 8

COACHING THE LONG JUMP AND THE TRIPLE JUMP

Because of the overlapping features of the long and triple jumps and because we combine both events in our coaching organization, it was decided to include these two events in one chapter to avoid certain obvious duplication. They are, however, two distinct events and I do not wish to imply otherwise by this chapter organization.

The selection of propects for these two events is made by a series of tests including sprinting, vertical reach, standing long and standing triple jumps. The latter is considered particularly important as it aids greatly in judging rhythm, coordination and leg strength. In the beginning we teach all selected prospects both events, separating them when we are able to determine where each individual's primary talent lies. The only exception to this would be with individuals who come to us from junior high with clearly demonstrated talent to become class long jumpers or runners. These individuals are not steered into the triple jump because of the wear and tear on the legs that event demands.

A. PRESENTING THE LONG JUMP
AND TRIPLE JUMP EVENTS

1. The long jump

As in field events we start with a classroom presentation of the events. Since the long jump techniques are utilized in both events, it makes sense to start by describing it. The first thing to explain to beginners is that the long jump is broken down into four stages: (1) the run-up or approach, (2) the take-off, (3) the flight, and (4) the landing or sit-out. It is also essential to stress at this point the importance of speed, but controlled speed, and the need for a uniform run. It must be emphasized that the secret of long jumping is the ability to direct all one's effort toward a vertical lift at take-off without losing speed. The athletes should be made to understand that what goes on in the air following take-off is significant, but is of minor importance in comparison to the run-up and take-off action. Explain that once an athlete leaves the ground there is nothing that individual can do to make the body travel farther. One can, however, prevent the body from coming down sooner—the purpose of the hang. I have found that youngsters understand this principle more readily if you use the analogy of a glider in flight; it will sail a long way but as soon as you aim the nose down, down it comes. The purpose of the hang is to avoid aiming the nose down too quickly.

The explanation of the long jump is concluded by a demonstration of the sit-out showing how a proper execution of this technique can add 18 inches to 2 feet to a jump as opposed to landing with the legs under the trunk. Finally, we re-emphasize priorities in long jump, speed and vertical lift at take-off.

2. The triple jump

In discussing the principles of triple jumping the first step is to be sure the youngsters actually understand the nature of the event. It is amazing how many really don't understand this event when they begin. Don't take it for granted they do. We first show them the concept of a hop-step-and jump and then explain where the term triple jump comes from. If properly executed the action is in reality after the take-off, One - Two - Three - Long Jump, with the foot not striking the ground on one. This is demonstrated on the blackboard, by walking through it and by loop films. It is extremely important to clarify this event in the beginner's mind before attempting to teach technique.

The key factor to stress once they understand the nature of the event is that it must be looked at as a whole and results are judged by overall distance achieved, not by distance in any single part. They must be aware that each stage must be completed in control before the next stage can begin, even though each stage should blend smoothly into the next. In particular, they must understand that maximum distance on the initial phase, the hop, will lead to counter-productive results on the step and jump. The teaching of this event will not be effective if the athlete fails to understand right from the beginning the importance of rhythm and the need to gain some degree of equality in all three phases.

B. TEACHING THE LONG JUMP AND TRIPLE JUMP

There are three basic areas to be taught in these events: (1) the uniform run-up, (2) long jumping technique, and (3) the techniques of the hop and step in triple jumping. Unlike most other events these do not have to be taught in progression and all three can be taught independently in the same practice session, eventually bringing them all together.

1. Determination of the jumping foot

Before you can do anything else, you must determine the jumping foot for each individual. In long jumping this is not a serious problem as it is simply a matter of determining what foot a youngster naturally takes off on when he or she jumps. If there is some indecision, use the vertical reach test to ascertain an individual's strongest jumping leg.

In the triple jump, however, there is a dilemma. The question is, should the strongest leg be used for the first two take-offs or should it be used for the long jump. I definitely prefer the stronger, stronger, weaker combination for triple jumpers. The problem is that if you teach it that way and it turns out a particular individual has greater talent in the long rather than the triple jump, then you have been teaching that youngster to long jump off his weaker leg. There is no one correct solution to this problem but there are four distinct alternatives that the coach should consider.

(1) Separate long jumping and triple jumping candidates right from the beginning. This solves the dilemma. The problem is that you can make an error in judgment and miss a great prospect in one event or the other if you put that individual in the wrong event.

(2) Teach all beginners until you have determined their primary event to long jump off both legs. This way you can get the ideal combination for both events. The problem is that you are complicating the process and confusing the beginner at a time when that is the last thing you want to do.

(3) Train everyone to hop and step off the weaker leg and long jump off the stronger, converting, if you think it is appropriate—and it may not be—when you determine an individual's primary event is going to be the triple jump.

(4) Train everyone to hop and step off the stronger leg and long jump off the weaker, converting when you determine an individual's primary event is going to be the long jump.

I do not recommend alternatives 1 or 2 although they certainly represent viable choices. My suggestion is to use your gut instinct as to whether or not an individual will be a better long or triple jumper. If it is the former, utilize alternative 3 and if it is the latter, utilize number 4. Don't ignore a youngster's strong preference either. Let him use whatever system he finds most comfortable. The important thing is to have a policy, not handle the problem arbitrarily.

2. The uniform run

The importance of this aspect of long and triple jumping can never be over-emphasized. An athlete who worries about hitting the board is never going to be successful. This phase has to become as smooth and natural as possible and this takes a great deal of time and effort. We start our prospects off with a 14-step run, counting every other step. An individual who takes off on the left foot will count seven lefts and those that jump off the right count seven rights. Counting every other step is much easier than counting them all and they *must* count at first. One has to take the same number of steps every time or the entire process is meaningless. It makes no difference what foot a jumper starts the run with; let him or her do whatever is most natural. A jumper who both starts the run and takes off on the same foot, starts counting on the first step. If it is more natural to start off on the opposite foot from the take-off one then simply add a step to the run and start counting lefts or rights on the second step. Keep this process as natural as you possibly can.

We send our jumpers off in partners, on the outside of the track somewhere, and have them work together on run-throughs. They always start from the same point and the partner counts the seven lefts or seven rights and marks where the seventh step lands. They keep repeating this process until they get the take-off point as consistent as possible. The coach should keep circulating while this is going on constantly stressing uniformity, relaxation and good sprinting technique. It is important not to attempt to work on this in adverse weather conditions. Eventually, jumpers must learn to adjust to adverse conditions, but in the beginning it is only going to lead to confusion and frustration in achieving a uniform and consistent run.

Once they have the approach run down reasonably well on the track, move them to the jumping runway. Keep the jumping technique work and the measured run-up separate in the teaching process. You must get the approach run down well before adding to it the distraction of the board and jumping. When we apply the approach to the runway we utilize two check marks. The first mark is the starting point and the second check represents the second counted left or right. The first four steps of the run are taken well under control and the second check mark is designed to give confidence in getting off to a good start. We do not use two checks in all field events that require an approach run but experience in the long and triple jump indicates this system works well for us in these events. There is no sacred one way to establish check marks. The coach should employ whatever system that he or she is most comfortable in using.

I have never advocated using checks further down the runway. It is much more difficult to execute a smooth uniform run while looking for check marks. The question is, also, if you miss a check well down the runway, what are you going to do about it? There is no way in the world an athlete can execute a good take-off if he or she is looking for a check and contemplating the possibility of stopping or adjusting stride if the check is missed.

The amont of speed generated on the approach run will vary for each individual. The more speed the better, provided it can be controlled. Control means simply being in position to execute an explosive take-off when one hits the board. We like to shoot for running at 90 percent of maximum speed down the runway but many jumpers cannot handle that. Triple jumpers have even a greater control problem and most cannot generate the same speed that long jumpers can. The coach must be the judge. If in your judgment an individual is not controlling the run, slow it down a bit.

The ideal length of the run is one that is just long enough to bring the athlete to maximum controllable speed at the point of take-off. As we progress, we lengthen the run until we arrive at what we feel is ideal for each individual. Be careful with this process. The longer the run, the more difficult it is to keep control and the easier it is to foul up the steps. Maximum efficiency in the jump is what you are looking for, nothing else. Invariably we find most long jumpers will end up with slightly longer runs than the triple jumpers because of the complexity and strain of the latter event.

3. Long jump technique

(1) The take-off

Although all great jumpers gather on the last two or three strides of the approach run, we do not teach it. Nor do we teach a shortening of the last stride or two. Both of these techniques tend to slow down a beginner considerably and throw the steps off. Usually, as a jumper progresses, the gather begins to take place naturally. If it doesn't, it is a refinement that can be readily worked on with an accomplished jumper. At this level it is most important to maintain speed and a uniform run right to the board. In the takeoff, vertical lift without losing speed should be emphasized. We tell our jumpers to drive the lead knee and opposite arm as high as they can, keeping the chest out and up, and getting as much height as possible. The plant involves a heel, ball, toe rotation, emphasizing as much force against the board with the planting foot as possible.(See Figure 8.1.)

A lot of short run pop-ups are effective in teaching takeoff. We have the athletes take a 3-6 stride run onto the board, concentrating on the takeoff action. We will also tie a string on two low hurdles and have them jump over the string to gain height. This is a good drill, but great care must be taken as to where the hurdles are placed. If they are too close to the board the youngster will slow down and end up high jumping. It is necessary to adjust the hurdle location for every individual. Be careful with this one, you can do more harm than good with improper placement.

(2) The hang or hitch kick

Although I believe the Hitch Kick is the better in-flight technique, this applies only to class jumpers. Consequently, we teach our beginners the hang. In my opinion the hang is a little easier to master, but, more important, most beginners simply cannot jump high enough and far enough to execute the hitch kick properly. Triple jumpers, particularly, are going to have extreme difficulty hitch-kicking in the long jump phase. Maybe the great ones can do it, but we have never had anyone that talented.

The purpose of a hang or hitch kick is to defy the law of gravity as long as possible. It is not to make the jumper go further but to prevent coming down sooner. In the hang the jumper arches the back, throws the head up with the arms up over the head and to the rear, with the legs bent back at the knees. The jumper holds this position until he or she begins to get the sensation of descending, and then snaps into the sit-out position. (See Figure 8.2.)

We use two drills to teach the hang. First, jumping off a Ruther Board onto a high jumping mat. The board gives the jumper a great deal of height and plenty of time to concentrate on the hang technique. Jumping into a high jump mat is more effective than into the long jump pit because when the latter is used there is a great temptation to see how far one can go and hence lose concentration on the purpose of the drill. A

FIGURE 8.1 Long Jump Take-off

FIGURE 8.2 Hang Position

second drill involves having the athlete stand on a Buck or small gymnastics horse and leap off it executing the hang.

If an accomplished jumper comes to us already doing the hitch kick we certainly make no effort to change him. Also, if we have an accomplished jumper indicate he wants to try the hitch we let him go ahead. If an accomplished jumper is content with the hang we stay with it. If we do go to the hitch kick, we teach a one and one-half step or run in the air, emphasizing keeping the body erect and bringing the arms up so they can snap into the sit-out position. The same drills used for the hang are also used for the hitch kick.

(3) The sit-out

An efficient sit-out landing adds considerably to a jump and can be the difference between an outstanding and average jumper. As the descent begins the athlete should bend forward with the trunk, bringing the legs up as close to being out straight as possible. The arms are extended to the front and the eyes are up. The athlete should begin to throw the arms back an instant before the heels hit the pit. As soon as the heels hit, the knees bend and the head comes down to prevent a falling back into the pit. A jumper may not have to worry about recovery when jumping into a superb pit, but that will seldom be the case in high school. We use the Ruther Board and the gymnastics horse in teaching and drilling on the sit-out, just as we do with the hang. (See Figure 8.3.)

FIGURE 8.3   Sit-out

(4) The hop and step technique of triple jumping

We initiate the teaching of the triple jump techniques by utilizing the standing hop, step and jump. It is vitally important in teaching the hop to emphasize that the athlete does not want to get maximum height. Stress getting the knee up high so the thigh of the lead leg is parallel to the ground, holding it there with the trunk in a vertical position. The jumper should think of a smooth running action in the air rather than a hopping action off the take-off leg. On take-off the foot lands almost flat-footed, but the heel does land first, in the same heel, ball and toe rotation we get in the long jump but without the upward force. The heel must land ahead of the body, so that the center of gravity rocks directly over the leg in contact with the ground. (See Figure 8.4.)

FIGURE 8.4 Hop Technique

In moving into the step, again the lead knee is brought up high bringing the thigh parallel to the ground, and the trail leg is back in two right angles. The legs and trunk should form what amounts to the bottom half of a swastika. The athlete holds this position as long as possible and literally sails through the air. In landing, you again want the foot slightly ahead of the body to bring the center of gravity over the take-off leg as the long jump take-off is executed. (See Figure 8.5.)

FIGURE 8.5   In-Flight Step Position

It is difficult to teach the hop separate from the step as one must blend smoothly into the other. It is important, however, to stress that one phase must be completed before moving into the next. The third phase is, of course, the long jump, the techniques of which have already been described. Obviously, what applies from the hop to the step applies here also. Unless the step is completed with good technique, there is no way in the world the athlete is going to have the momentum and control necessary to achieve anything resembling a decent long jump.

The hop is a great deal easier to execute than the step, probably because it comes first, and the problem is to keep the hop down and under control so a proper step can be accomplished. One drill we use is to move the take-off point closer to the pit and execute the hop and step, holding the sail through the air position of the step and landing that way into the pit. Another drill for the step is called the "Gazelle." This is a bounding type action from one leg to the other, sailing through the air in the mid-flight step position. The Gazelles are usually done up and down the football field, but we also do them up the stadium stairs, and synchronized with rope jumping. Another drill involves executing the hop, step and jump over three hurdles about 15 feet apart, allowing the athlete to take two running strides in between each phase. As we progress with this drill we shorten the distance between the hurdles and eliminate the running strides in between.

I have deliberately avoided discussing arm action up to this point. We believe in the double arm action but do not teach it until the athletes have the hop, step and jump technique down reasonably well. It is our experience that if an attempt is made to teach the double arm action right from the beginning it only confuses the issue. Triple jumping is a very difficult process and adding sophisticated arm action too early can be counter-productive. Initially, we let the arms take care of themselves, correcting only flagrant flaws that throw the athlete off balance. Only when we judge the athlete ready do we introduce the double arm action by walking through it and then gradually speeding up the process. This should be accomplished well before the competitive season commences. If you haven't introduced the double arm action to a key athlete who is scoring points for you once he gets into competition, it is best to leave it for another year.

In teaching the double arm action, the concept to get across is that both arms swing back and forth simultaneously in all three phases of the triple jump sequence. Also, in the double arm action, although the hop and step phases must still be controlled, a slightly greater height should be attained in both the hop and step phases. Prior to the planting of the take-off foot, both arms are swung back almost parallel to the ground and just before the plant of the take-off foot they are swung forward, reaching upward as though reaching for a high bar at eye level. They are then withdrawn in a circular motion and dropped to waist level behind the body to prepare for the gather and planting for the step. Again, just before the planting foot lands the arms reach forward and upward as described above, only with a slight forward body lean at this stage. The arms are again withdrawn as in the hop in preparation for the jump. In the jump, just as the heel makes contact an instant before the full foot lands, the arms are swept forward and high in line with the body. At the height of the jump they are thrown back in the hang and then forward for the sit-out.

5. Sequence in triple jumping

I am firmly convinced there is not one perfect hop, step and jump sequence for all triple jumpers. Copying the sequence of a world class performer may not be wise for the high school jumper. This is a matter that definitely has to be worked out on an individual basis. We tell our youngsters to keep the height of the hop and the height of the step as equal as possible and the length of each also as equal as they can. Ideally, the step should be slightly higher than the hop but it is the rare high school athlete, indeed, who will ever do it. Invariably, the problem will be in the opposite direction. The challenge is to get the step as close as we can to the hop. When they get to the jump, they should strive to get as high and as far out as they can, but without cutting down on the step to do it.

It takes a great deal of analysis for each individual triple jumper. I strongly recommend seeking equality in all three phases until you are sure of what constitutes a particular individual's best ratio or sequence. At that point it is advantageous to utilize markers as targets for each phase. Again, don't do this arbitrarily or based upon some world class jumper's ratio. Until you are sure, stick to emphasizing rhythm, smoothness and equality in each phase.

C. TRAINING LONG JUMPERS
AND TRIPLE JUMPERS

1. Technique training

The long jump, more than any other event, involves coaching overlap. Because of the importance of speed in long jumping, sprinters and hurdlers frequently participate in the event as a secondary activity. With real class long jumpers the opposite is often true. It is the task of the head coach to coordinate the practice schedules for athletes who fall in either category. Those who are primarily long jumpers spend all the practice sessions with the jumping coach except for the running portions of the workouts, which are supervised by the hurdling and sprinting coaches. Those whose first concentration is in a running area are channeled to the jumping coach during technique work and spend the bulk of the practice under the supervision of the running event coach. It is not good policy to go 50 − 50, as the best you can hope for is a 50 percent jumper. All our long jumpers concentrate on a primary area and either jump or run in the other for what we like to call gravy points.

The triple jump, however, represents a very different story. Triple jumping is a very demanding event that puts a tremendous amount of strain on the legs. It requires extensive leg strength and for this reason it is our policy not to triple jump an individual as a second event. An athlete who is a class runner or a class long jumper is going to suffer in his primary event if he is used in the triple jump. As a result, all our triple jumpers compete in this event as their primary area. We have triple jumpers running and long-jumping for points but never runners or long jumpers triple-jumping for points.

In training long and triple jumpers practice sessions are divided into five basic areas: (1) work on the run-up or approach, (2) technique development and drills, (3) actual jumping, (4) running workouts, and (5) strength training. We devote a 15-minute segment at the beginning of each week just to re-emphasize the techniques of smooth, relaxed, uniform running. Prior to the competitive season a little time should be devoted to this in every practice. Twice a week during the competitive season, preferably the practices preceding competition or measured jumping, a good solid 30-minute session working on the measured run should be incorporated.

The first day of each week is the day devoted to extensive technique work and drilling. In our particular situation we often have dual meets scheduled on Wednesdays and multi-school competition on Saturday. When this is the case, these two sessions represent the total of our full measured run jumping for the week. If there is no midweek dual meet, we will usually take six all-out jumps in practice on Wednesdays.

The extent of the Tuesday workout will depend on the degree of challenge on Wednesday. If we are facing an extremely important league dual meet, it makes little sense not to have our jumpers as rested as possible. Under normal conditions, however, we like to have a full, although not a strenuous, workout on Tuesdays with some technique drilling that will not be tough on the jumper. Thursday is always a tapering off day with primary emphasis upon perfecting the approach run and building confidence for the competition coming up on Saturday.

The day before competition is always a day of rest or possibly some light loosening up, depending upon the preference of the individual. Jumpers do not have unlimited spring in their legs and should always be well rested before competition. Obviously, if you are faced with a lot of meets you could find yourself always resting and competing, with very little time for practice. There are times when you are simply going to have to train right through certain meets if you want to have your jumpers ready for major competition at the end of the season. If you have the talent that enables you to win anyway, this is not difficult to do. When you have just average talent and have to struggle to win every meet, then it becomes a matter of priorities.

2. Strength training

In the off-season and the early regular season all long jump-triple jumpers work on a three-sessions per-week schedule utilizing the regular workout concept described in Chapter 2. As soon as the competitive season begins we cut back to a twice weekly regular-explosive sequence. Whenever possible on alternate days we do three sets of 10 on the Leaper Machine as well as regular sprint drills with the weight jacket. Great care should be taken never to do this type of work the day before competition and in most cases with long jump-triple jumpers we have found it wise to stay away from it two days prior to a major meet or serious challenge.

Free Weight Workout:	Weight Machine Workout:
Heel raises	Heel raises (Free weights)
Squats	Squats (Free weights)
Leg extensions (Machine)	Leg extensions
Leg curls (Machine)	Leg curls
Inclined sit-ups	Inclined sit-ups
Leg lifts	Leg lifts
Bench press	Dips
Military press	Front trunk twists
Forearm curls	Bench press
Upright rowing	Military press
	Forearm curls
	Upright rowing
	Kneeling pulldowns

3. Running workouts

Those individuals who long-jump as a secondary event do all their running work with their regular sprint or hurdles coach. Those whose primary concentration is jumping will follow a similar, though reduced, program with our sprinters. All long jumpers and triple jumpers need sprinting speed and are trained accordingly. We do a lot of uphill and downhill running, Whistlers for relaxation and anaerobic workouts as described in the chapter on sprinting. Jumpers should do a minimum of 30 minutes of running work in every regular practice session.

D. ANALYZING THE MOST COMMON FAULTS IN HIGH SCHOOL LONG AND TRIPLE JUMPING

1. Long jumping

(1) Loss of momentum

i. *Cause:* The major cause of loss of momentum in the approach run is tension and the inability to maintain relaxation. Most often this is the result of trying too hard and putting the effort in the wrong place.

ii. *Correction:* It is imperative that young jumpers understand they can run faster relaxed than they can by straining and they must run no differently in meets than they do in practice. Another way of putting this is that they must not lose their poise. Constant work on steps, uniform running, rhythm and relaxation must be a part of the training program from the first day of the season until the last. Never take this for granted. If necessary, get the jumper with a serious momentum problem away from the pit for this type of work, just as was recommended in the teaching process.

(2) Improper take-off

i. *Cause:* The two major culprits in a poor take-off are looking for the board at the end of the approach and thinking out rather than up when the take-off is initiated.

ii. *Correction:* The fear of fouling is a major psychological barrier that must be overcome in long jumping. Unless you are dealing with a superstar against inferior competition, no one is going to get very far in long jumping looking for the board. Repeated work on uniform running and on the measured approach is essential in order to build a youngster's confidence in hitting the board. It is important to condition them to expect fouls and not to panic if one takes place in competition. In particularly troublesome cases, try having the youngster run through and jump blindfolded. They will be a little squeamish at first, but it is not dangerous and can be a very effective tool in developing confidence in the run-up and thinking proper take-off.

More often than not the jumper who thinks out rather than up just does not understand the mechanics of the event. In the section on teaching take-off we described drills for this technique and they should be constantly utilized, even for jumpers who take off properly. The chances are, however, that the jumper who is not getting height is thinking where he or she wants to end up rather than the proper route of getting there.

(3) Coming down too soon once in flight

i. *Cause:* Failure to execute the hang or hitch kick properly is going to result in the jumper's nosing down before he or she has to.

ii. *Correction* The cause of a poor hang or hitch kick is the loss of momentum in the approach and a poor take-off. If one doesn't get up in the air properly, there will simply not be time for a good hang or hitch kick. Further, many jumpers are over-anxious and thrust the legs out in front as soon as they leave the ground. They are actually attempting to sit-out before they really get started. Others will get into the hang properly and then lose their timing and snap into the sit-out too quickly. Patience to remain in the hang or hitch kick until the descent begins is essential to maximum jumping efficiency. The Ruther Board drills described in the teaching process are very helpful in executing and timing a proper hang or hitch kick.

(4) Failure to execute the sit-out

i. *Cause:* More often than not the failure to execute a good sit-out is the result of faults committed in the early stages of the event. One has to get up there and stay there in order to be able to pick up the extra distance a good sit-out represents.

ii. *Correction:* Drilling off the Ruther Board on proper sit-out form will help, but the real emphasis must come in working on the earlier stages. If a youngster is not sitting-out, concentrate upon take-off and hang; the sit-out will come.

2. Triple jump

The problems of loss of momentum and the problems of long jumping just described are equally applicable to triple jumping and will not be repeated.

(1) Getting too much height and distance on the hop

i. *Cause:* The youngster is thinking too much like a long jumper. He is over-emphasizing the high knee action at take-off and trying to get too much height.

ii. *Correction:* The most important factor here is to be sure the athlete understands and is convinced of the fact that maximum effort on the hop is going to be counter-productive in the triple jump as a whole. This is why it makes good sense not to drill on the hop alone but to combine it with the step as much as possible. Drill the triple jumpers on about a 20-degree angle of take-off. Setting a marker out to shoot for in the hop is very beneficial even if you have not determined an ideal sequence or ratio of hop, step and jump. You can estimate what you think the athlete ought to be jumping and set the marks out at one-third the distance.

(2) Too short a step

i. *Cause:* Invariably, too short a step is caused by too long or too high a hop. Another factor could be that the athlete is over anxious to get into the long jump phase.

ii. *Correction:* Combining drills on the hop and step is the best way to keep the step out where it belongs. The drill described in the teaching process where the jumper sails through the air in the step phase and lands in the midair position in the pit is an extremely good way to improve the step. The Gazelle drills are also beneficial in this regard, but the real culprit in a poor step is getting too much out of the hop.

(3) Loss of control of body during hop and step action

i. *Cause:* Loss of control of the body results in a pronounced forward lean or in the body's bouncing from side to side. Loss of control is the result of over-anxiousness and straining.

ii. *Correction:* Like pole vaulting, triple jumping is a progression event. It is absolutely essential to keep the body erect and the center of gravity over the take-off legs in each of the three phases. Once a youngster starts to get anxious and leans forward, the problem gets progressively worse as the event progresses. The key is drilling on smoothness, rhythm and equality in the phases. Again, if a youngster is shooting for properly placed markers, the tendency to lean forward for more distance is greatly reduced.

Often you will never realize a youngster is bouncing from side to side unless the event is observed from either the front or the rear. Again, the key is drilling on smoothness, rhythm and equality. Blindfolded triple jumping is again beneficial in dealing with this problem as control is usually lost by a desire to see where one is going and to get there too quickly.

Since controlled speed is such a vital factor in long jumping, failure to maintain control when reaching the long jump phase in triple jumping is absolutely fatal. The hop and step action is going to reduce speed considerably even with the best. If an individual does not come out of the step under control, the long jump is doomed.

E. SPECIAL PROBLEMS IN COACHING
GIRL LONG JUMPERS

Unfortunately, triple jumping is not a girl's event in Massachusetts and I simply have no experience with girls in this area. Frankly, I can understand the reasoning behind girls not pole vaulting or high hurdling, but I see no reason why there is a reluctance to include the triple jump in their program. What the girls lack in leg strength they make up in coordination and rhythm. I think it would be an excellent event for girls and have campaigned accordingly for some time.

As far as long jumping is concerned, there really is no justification for treating girls any differently from boys or for teaching any different techniques. It seems that jumping in the 15-17 foot range, as most high school girls do, would preclude considering the hitch kick over the hang. Possibly one might consider a slightly shorter approach run for girls but only if the girl does not have a good athletic background. If the girl is well trained, there is no reason why she cannot handle as long a run-up as the boys, since speed is relative and the girls are not going to reach maximum controllable speed any quicker than the boys.

What was said in the chapter on high jumping regarding weight and body development is equally applicable to girls in long jumping. There is no need to repeat that explanation except to re-emphasize the importance of good dieting habits and the need to start girl long jumpers early.

SAMPLE LONG JUMP—TRIPLE JUMP WORK WEEK (MID-SEASON)

Monday:

30 Min. Flexibility and warm-up
15 Min. Work on uniform running
30 Min. Long jump technique drills (Pop-ups, hang drills, sit outs)
30 Min. Triple jump technique drills (Standing triple jumps, hop and step drills, step drill into pit etc.)
        Long jumpers'—4 × 220's 90%
15 Min. 10 × uphills
45 Min. Regular weight workout (Advanced)
        Rope skipping and leaper machine (Beginners)

Tuesday:

30 Min. Flexibility and warm-up
30 Min. Run-throughs working on steps
15 Min. Long jumpers' Pop-ups
        Triple jumpers' Gazelle drills

Tuesday: (*cont.*)

15 Min. Long jumpers' 10 × downhill running
          Triple jumpers Hop and step drill over hurdles
15 Min. Weight jacket drills
45 Min. Rope skipping and leaper machine (Advanced)
          Regular weight workout (Beginners)

Wednesday:

30 Min. Flexibility and warm-up
45 Min. Full run all out jumping
30 Min. 6 × Whistlers (relaxation sprinting)
45 Min. Explosive weight workout (Advanced)
          Rope skipping and leaper machine (Beginners)

Thursday:

30 Min. Flexibility and warm-up
30 Min. Run-throughs working on steps
15 Min. Pop-ups
15 Min. 10 × downhill running
15 Min. 10 × uphill running
45 Min. Rope skipping and leaper machine (Advanced)
          Explosive weight workout (Beginners)

Friday:

Rest or optional light loosening workout (Advanced)

Goal Day (Beginners)

Saturday:

Competition

CHAPTER 9

COACHING THE POLE VAULT

The most difficult event in track and field, from the point of view of the athlete, coach and budget is the Pole Vault. It is a beautiful event, however, whose proper execution combines a unique blend of speed, strength, agility, timing and courage. It is financially expensive and can be very dangerous if not carefully and competently supervised. A school not willing to make a full commitment to running the event properly should not include it in its track and field program.

A. SELECTING POLE VAULT PROSPECTS

Testing for prospects in the pole vault is a very important process and requires more care than testing in other events. One can readily select athletes with the needed physical requirements through speed, strength and gymnastic ability tests. The most important ingredients, however, desire and courage, cannot be tested so easily. I strongly believe you cannot really judge potential in the pole vault without actually putting your youngsters on the pole. Our kids call the pole vault test "Kamikaze Day." This is the one test we do not require everybody to take. If a youngster indicates he does not want to be tested for the pole vault, we do not force him and we do not embarrass him by making a case about it in front of the team. We also eliminate from the testing process certain physical types who could not possibly ever participate in the vault.

The most important factor in the pole vault test is safety. We surround the pit with as many as 10 people, as far as possible our experienced vaulters, and utilize them as spotters. We briefly show the youngsters being tested how to hold the pole, run up and plant, and then let it go. The pole vault coach stands directly at the planting box, grabbing the pole on each attempt and bringing it up to the vertical. What we are looking for is instinct and courage. The pole vault coach is the judge. If he feels an individual attacks the vault eagerly and shows a physical aptitude for it, that youngster is put on the beginners list. If the eagerness is not there, the individual is not selected, even if in possession of certain advantageous physical characteristics. Have a little flexibility in this process, however. If some youngster comes to you with a passionate plea to be a pole vaulter, let him stay with the beginners, unless you feel he could be seriously hurt, at least until you have a little more evidence. Likewise, if someone you select indicates a desire not to be included, do not force him.

What you have accomplished in the testing process is to select those individuals to whom you will attempt to teach the vault. In some years we have selected as many as 15 youngsters to go into this beginners' group. Many of these never made our pole vaulting squad as the individuals with real potential in this event did not begin to separate from the pack until some real teaching had taken place. What the testing process accomplishes is to put together a group of youngsters with potential who want to be vaulters. I strongly re-emphasize—do not force anyone into this event.

B. PRESENTING THE EVENT

In the pole vault our beginners have had more introduction to the event than their counterparts in other areas due to the testing process. Nevertheless, once they are selected we bring them into a classroom presentation. The first thing we do is show them loop films of top vaulters in action in order to establish an appreciation of what a proper vault is like. It is very important right here in the beginning to make clear the basic principle involved in vaulting. It is particularly vital that the youngsters understand the function of the pole. Most beginners think of the pole as a brace with which the vaulter pulls himself over the bar. That notion must be dispelled right from the start and the athlete should fully understand the pole is a vehicle upon which he will ride up to the bar. They must understand that the pole has to reach a vertical position in order for the vaulter to be close enough to the bar for clearance when he leaves the pole. We demonstrate with an old pole or stick how pulling on the pole causes it to come back to the ground. Explain to them that you will teach them to run up, plant, take off and ride the pole properly so that it will reach that absolutely essential vertical position. Also, explain the bending feature of the fiberglass pole and show them how this will increase propulsion into the verical position. It is absolutely essential that a beginner understand the function of the pole if any subsequent teaching is going to have meaning.

The other objective of the classroom session is to make the beginners aware that the vault is made up of distinct stages. Don't go into detail at this point but simply make them aware how the run-up, plant, take-off, swing, rock back, drive-turn-push and fly away all blend together into one smooth operation, but with each stage being completed before the next stage begins. As in all field events, as you teach each stage individually, it is important the athlete understands how it fits into the total picture.

C. TEACHING THE POLE VAULT

1. The carry and run

Begin the teaching process by showing the youngsters how to hold and carry the pole. We have them stand with the pole vertical and reach up grabbing the pole as high as they can with the bottom or left hand. Bring the pole then down to the waist and grasp it with the right or top hand so that there is roughly three inches of daylight between the hips and the hands on each side. This will give them approximately a 24-inch hand spread. Have them turn the top hand away from the body and the lower hand toward the body. The left hand and thumb act as a fulcrum with the thumb supporting a majority of the pole's weight. Tell them to apply pressure downward with the right hand and thumb. The hands should grip the pole firmly but not tightly. Obviously, the above hand position is for beginners. As the athlete becomes more proficient the hand hold is raised according to that individual's ability to handle it.

In the run-up we teach our vaulters to carry the pole with the tip slightly higher than the head. It is much easier to execute the carry if the vaulter brings the tip of the pole as high as a 45-to 50-degree angle and starts the run-up as the pole reaches its weightless point. As the run starts, begin to lower the tip by raising the right hand. The pole should be in the slightly higher than eye level carry position by the completion of the first three steps. Teach the prospective vaulter to run as much like a sprinter as possible with the arms relaxed, the shoulders square and the pole in control. Beginners should do a tremendous amount of running with the pole. They must develop as uniform a running stride as they possibly can. We tell them, "Think like a musician, play it the same way every time." Even if you are coaching in an area where weather conditions force you into a late start and if you do not have indoor facilities, you can still spend a great deal of time running with the pole and have that process well down prior to actually working at the vaulting pit.

2. The plant

The next step, the teaching of the plant, is one of the real keys of vaulting. First show them the flex point of the pole and explain that to get proper bend from the pole the flex point should be planted at 11 o'clock as the pole strikes the box. Most poles have the flex point marked on them, but, if not, you can find it and mark it yourself by placing the pole on two hurdles, eight feet apart, rolling the pole and letting it settle. When the pole settles the flex point will be facing the ground.

Start off by walking through the plant. We use the curl-press style plant because we have found by experience it to be more successful than the overhead style formerly utilized. The plant takes place on the last two steps of the run-up, although the vaulter should think plant a step or two earlier. On the next to last stride the right hand comes upward-outward and inward to the right ear. On the last stride tell the vaulter to drive or lift the right hand from the ear straight up so that if the pole came down it would split his head in half. We tell the vaulters to shoot for the pole's hitting the back of the box simultaneously with the final step (left foot for right-handed vaulters) striking the ground. Have them walk through this process at first, then jog it, gradually increasing speed of the run-up until the timing and synchronization of the plant are mastered. This is another area that can be worked on extensively before weather conditions permit the use of the vaulting area. A device known as the Simplant is very useful in teaching the plant. This device is a box that sits on the floor or ground and slides when the plant is made. It enables the vaulter to effectively work on plant and run through without the jarring that results from a stationary box. (See Figure 9.1.)

3. The measured run-up and take-off point

Since a proper take-off point is absolutely essential to the rest of the vaulting process, the athlete must have a uniform measured run-up, even

FIGURE 9.1   Position at Pole Plant

if it is a very short one, before attempting an actual vault. Move the vaulters out on the track in pairs, use one to mark while the other runs through.
We start our beginners with an eight-step run, which will be sufficient
because we will not be utilizing a bar in our early vaulting. Always starting from the same point, one partner runs through and the other marks
where the eighth step lands. The process is repeated over and over until
the eighth step is striking the ground consistently in the same place.

　　Once the run is down, move back to the runway and establish the
take-off point. Have the vaulter place the pole in the planting box with the
top hand directly over the head and in a straight line with the trunk and
take-off foot. Mark the position of the take-off foot, measure back the
distance determined in the run-throughs and make this the beginning
starting mark.

　　As each vaulter becomes more proficient, the length of the run is increased gradually. We have no set length of run for our pole vaulters as each individual's ability to sustain controlled speed carrying a pole will vary significantly. The more speed the better, but only if the athlete is in complete control and can execute the plant and take-off properly. It is a serious mistake to predetermine the length of a vaulter's run and the speed he should attempt to generate. Gradually increase both speed and length of run as the vaulter improves until both you and he are satisfied that they best suit his needs at that particular moment. We do not use a second check mark with vaulters, although there is no serious quarrel with those who do, as we believe a second check down the runway is a distraction. Running properly carrying a pole and executing a proper plant and take-off is a great deal more difficult than hitting a long jump board. A vaulter's full concentration must be on the plant and take-off.

4. Pole selection

Up to this point you can place any sort of pole in the vaulters' hands in the teaching process. Once they are ready for take-off, however, care must be taken in pole selection. All fiberglass vaulting poles are designed according to the weight of the vaulter, and, in some cases, according to how high the pole is held. This information is made available with every pole and should be scrupulously followed. If you put a youngster on a pole that is too heavy, he is not going to be able to handle it. If you put him on one that is designed for a vaulter of lesser weight, the pole can easily break and cause serious injury. Don't give in to the temptation of putting a youngster on a pole designed for a lighter vaulter because it bends more easily and may get him over lower heights more readily in the beginning. If the vault is executed correctly, a properly weighted pole will provide the most effective bend. Using a light pole is definitely not worth the risk.

5. The take-off

In teaching the take-off, emphasize a good knee lift, just as in long jumping. We tell our vaulters, "Run through the box and think like a long jumper." By far this is the most critical aspect of the vault. I have heard experts say at clinics that the run-up, plant and take off represent 90 percent of the vault and merit 90 percent of your teaching and attention. If the athlete slows down on the run-up, misses the take-off point, plants too early or too late, or fails to drive through the pole and into the pit on the take-off, he is not going to have pole speed and good bend. Without these ingredients, the pole is not going to reach the vertical and anything done from this point on is not going to make much difference. Spend your time on these areas. Don't worry particularly about the rest of the vaulting action until you can get the youngster off the ground properly.

6. Riding the pole

Once off the ground, emphasize riding with the pole. Stress not to consciously try to bend the pole. The left arm should be bent and the right arm straight. The pole should remain at the same distance from the body throughout the riding phase. As the pole bends, the eyes should go with it. You are looking basically for the same action as swinging from a rope out over the old swimming hole. We drill on this action a great deal in the gym, swinging out on a rope and hanging. As the hips are swung up, the left, or take-off leg, catches up with the right. It is very important not to rush into the rock-back position. Tell the athlete to hang well behind the pole and get the hips and left leg up. When the rock-back takes place, it should be in a quick, fluid motion with the head and shoulders rocking back as one unit, not separately. (See Figure 9.2.)

This is the point in the vault that takes the greatest amount of courage. The athlete must lie there on his back as the pole unbends. We tell the vaulters that when they feel they are going to fall backward they are in the correct position. The average youngster is simply not going to be able to do this. It takes a lot of spunk and a unique individual, but if you have the right person, he will do it. (See Figure 9.3.)

While on the back, the feet start upward and the vaulter should try to get the knees up over the hips and shoot for the top of the pole. It should also be emphasized that the arms should not collapse; tell the vaulter to hold on and ride.

7. The turn and bar clearance

As the pole begins to reach the vertical, tell your vaulter to bring the right leg over the left in a scissors turn and drive the right arm down, an action that begins to turn the shoulders. Tell him to continue to drive down on the pole as long as he can before releasing with the left hand first and then finally pushing off with the right. The term most often used to describe this action is the "pull-turn and push." We never use this expression. We never use the term "pull" because we do not want our vaulters ever to think pull as this will almost inevitably result in a premature pulling of the pole somewhere along the line.

FIGURE 9.2   Arm Position—Pole Ride

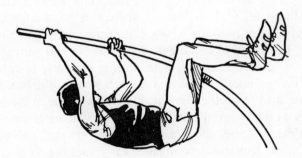

FIGURE 9.3   Rock Back Position

The action over the bar is a simple fly away. Tell the vaulter to bring the thumb in toward the body, lifting the hands straight up and hollowing the chest. (See Figure 9.4.)

FIGURE 9.4   Fly-Away Position

8. Two key coaching points

i. Teach the vault without the use of a crossbar. What goes on before the athlete gets to the bar is much more important than what takes place at the top of the pole. With the bar up, there is a definite tendency for the athlete to give priority to the wrong end of the vault. There is also a real fear among beginners of coming down on the bar and getting hurt. It is a good idea to remove these obstacles during the early learning process.

ii. With beginners, we have the coach stand at the box and grab the pole helping it to reach the vertical, just as was done in the testing process. This is a controversial coaching tactic as you are obviously cheating for the athlete. What is accomplished, however, is the elimination of a great deal of the fear that accompanies early vaulting. It also enables the young vaulter to carry the entire process through. Young vaulters should be weaned from this assistance as soon as possible, but we find that it gives them confidence in the beginning and hastens the learning process. Stalling out represents a great fear of vaulters, especially beginners, and is the cause of serious injuries. Our beginners know they are not going to stall out because the coach is there to help the pole up. The more we do this, the more we tell the vaulters, "I did not help you much that time." As soon as possible we tell the vaulters that we will not grab the pole, but will be there and do so if it is necessary. Eventually, the coach gets out of there altogether, but only when both the coach and athlete are confident of the latter's ability to get off the ground and ride the pole.

9. Drills for the action at the top of the pole

Vaulters should do a lot of drilling on the action at the top of the pole because, even with the coach helping with the pole, the beginner is frequently going to make errors in the early stages of the vault and seldom ever get to the top of the pole action. One drill we use involves a rope in the gym. Tell the youngster to grab the rope, jump up and get upside down (only to get on the rope) and then execute the scissors action and the downward drive of the arm. We do the same thing on a pole held vertical by a partner or on the football goal post. The most successful drill for the top of the pole action, however, is what we call the Butt Burner. Have the vaulter sit on the floor, the waxed corridors of the school work the best, with a towel under him. The pole is lying on the floor on the left side of the vaulter, jammed into the wall. The vaulter sits facing away from the pole tip and the wall. Have him hold the pole just as he would at the top of the vault and drive hard into the pole, sliding on the towel and pivoting into the scissors action at the top of the pole. All of our vaulters feel this simulates the action at the top of the pole better than any other drill we have tried. It is very important in any drill of this nature to work on only one action. It is extremely difficult, if not impossible, to simulate in any drill the combining of more than one action of the entire vault.

D. TRAINING THE HIGH SCHOOL VAULTER

1. Technique training

Developing pole vaulters in areas like New England is very difficult. At best we can hope for two months of outdoor vaulting and in some years, when we have a late spring and April blizzards, the best we can hope for is six to seven weeks of decent outdoor vaulting conditions. As a result we built a wooden runway and installed a planting box in it in such a manner that it is put together in sections and can be readily dismantled so as not to interfere with gym classes. Actually, we got the specifications and idea from an outstanding rival coach in our league. With less than ideal weather conditions it is almost impossible to develop class pole vaulters without the benefit of some sort of indoor facility. If such a facility is not possibe, you can at least get the vaulters started with pole running, planting with the Simplant and gymnasium drills.

As in the high jump, we like to work our pole vaulters in practice at heights slightly below their maximum achievement. With the vaulters we like to work six inches to one foot below their best. When the vaulter goes for height he should be rested just as he would be for competition. Don't tax a vaulter to the limit if he is not physically and psychologically ready for the challenge. All you will accomplish is failure and a weakening of his confidence to make that particular height. At practice, also, don't keep the vaulter at a height at which he is constantly failing. Either lower the bar a bit to a height at which he can succeed, or stop vaulting on that day. The pole vaulter and the high jumper both face the psychological phenomenon of the failure message every time they knock the bar off the standards. It is difficult to teach and develop technique in an atmosphere of failure. This is another reason we like to vault our beginners without a bar.

Just as we explained in the high jump chapter, it is important in the pole vault to make a sound coaching judgment as to whether or not an athlete should continue vaulting after winning a competition. Without repeating all the reasoning described in the high jump chapter, it sometimes makes good sense to stop when ahead if the coach believes the athlete has peaked for the day, rather than leave with the taste of three misses in his mouth. Don't hold him back if he really wants to keep going and you feel conditions are favorable, but don't always keep going until failure takes place.

Pole vaulters must be in superb physical condition. Not only must they have speed, strength and agility, they must sustain these qualities over extremely long periods of time. I have seen pole vault competitions last for six hours or more in major meets. With the exception of the decathlon, no other event in track and field can match the pole vault in duration of competition. When the vaulter needs his physical capacities the most, when the gets to the ultimate heights of the competition, is the time when he is most seriously faced with both mental and physical fatigue. In view of these factors the pole vaulter must be well rested before competition, but, on the other hand, to be ready he must train to the ultimate in practice.

2. Strength training

Pole vaulters must be involved in a year-round weight training program, even if involved in other sports as most of our vaulters are. We put our vaulters through the same standard weight training program that we give to our competitors in the weight events. We also like to work them on the leaper machine as we do our jumpers. Our vaulters lift three times a week whenever possible, adjusting only to our rule of never lifting the day before competition. With some vaulters you may want to consider staying away from the weights two days before a major meet, depending on the individual. Our vaulters lift heavy the first workout of the week and regular the rest of the week as described in the section on weight training. Once we get into the actual competitive season we drop the heavy workouts and utilize a regular-regular-explosive sequence.

Gymnastic exercises of all types should also be a part of the pole vaulters' strength and agility training. We do a lot of rope climbing and ring work particularly. We have been fortunate down through the years to have a number of the members of the school's gymnastics team on our pole vaulting squad. I cannot think of a better preparation for the vault than a full season of competitive gymnastics prior to a season of vaulting.

Free Weight Workout:	Weight Machine Workout:
Bench press	Bench press
Military press	Military press
Inclined press	Inclined press
Squats	Front trunk twists
Heel raises	Forearm curls
Clean and jerk	Upright rowing
Forearm curls	Kneeling pulldowns
Upright rowing	Dips
Inclined sit-ups	Leg press
Leg lifts	Inclined sit-ups
Leg extensions	Leg lifts
Leg curls	Leg Extensions
	Leg curls

3. Running workouts

Pole vaulters should go through as rigorous a running workout schedule as possible. We never let a practice day go by without a good solid running workout for the pole vaulters. Pole vaulters should do exactly the same type of work as the sprinters and quarter milers. This means uphill and downhill running, relaxation sprints, anaerobic repeat 220's and 330's as well as a great deal of work developing a uniform stride and running with the pole. In addition, the vaulters should get out twice a week for a conditioning cross-country run and should do even more of this type of work in the off-season. As previously stated, endurance is a major factor in pole vaulting and it should not be neglected in the training program.

E. ANALYZING THE MOST COMMON FAULTS IN HIGH SCHOOL POLE VAULTING

1. Improper approach run to the box

This fault will result in either a slowing down as the vaulter reaches the take-off point or in taking off too close or too far from the bar.

i. Cause

A number of factors can lead to an inefficient approach run. Probably, the main culprit is a lack of confidence on the part of the vaulter causing him to lose uniformity in stride. Overstriding to the box is very common among high school vaulters. Carelessness in the pole carry and failure to keep the shoulders square are common factors that will destroy the approach.

ii. Correction

The key here is extensive practicing on the uniform run, concentrating on running the same number of steps in exactly the same manner every time. If necessary, get the vaulters away from the vaulting area when working on this. Running with a pole is very difficult. All vaulters, especially inexperienced ones, must do a great deal of drilling on it.

In competition this may necessitate moving the starting mark back or forward, provided the run-up has been smooth and consistent. If weather and the runway surface are the problem, then adjustments must be made. If the approach run has lost consistency and uniformity, however, adjusting the mark might well do more harm than good.

2. Improper take-off

i. Cause 1

Failure to time the plant correctly can cause havoc with the take-off. If the plant starts too soon, it results in stabbing at the box or "harpooning" it. The vaulter will be taking off too far behind his top hand. If the plant is too late, the vaulter ends up too close to the box and gets whipped underneath.

ii. Correction

Planting too late can be a jolting experience and vaulters are not prone to repeating it. Planting too soon, however, is much more common. Either way, you must go back to drilling on the plant, even going back to walking through the process if necessary. Very important also is to recognize that if the run-up is off, the plant wil be also. The cause of a poor plant may well be a poor approach and that is where the correction emphasis should be directed.

i. Cause 2

A poor take-off can also be caused by failing to get the pole directly over the head at the moment of take-off. This is usually caused by rushing into the vault. The vaulter is over-anxious and wants to get off the ground too quickly.

ii. Correction

Again it is necessary to go back to the run-up and the plant. A good tactic to consider here is eliminating the crossbar for a while, allowing the vaulter to concentrate better on the plant and take-off timing.

i. Cause 3

This is almost exclusively a problem among beginners, but there are times when the problem results from taking off on the wrong foot.

ii. Correction

Our experience has been that this possibility is most often overlooked. It happens with beginners and it is something you should be aware of and guard against. Again, go back to the approach and the plant drills.

3. Stalling of the pole

Stalling of the pole is another way of saying the vaulter has failed to bring the pole to the vertical position. It is the most serious of all vaulting faults because it can lead to landing other than in the pit with the possibility of injury.

i. Cause 1

The major cause of stalling is a breakdown of the earlier stages of the vault. Loss of momentum in the run-up, a poor plant and consequently a poor take-off, all can lead to stalling.

ii. Correction

If a youngster is stalling, the first thing you should do is to go back to drilling on the run, plant and take-off. This is a significant example of the statement made earlier that 90 percent of coaching time should be spent in these areas. In pole vaulting it is important to deal with the cause and not the effect.

i. Cause 2

Even with a good take-off, a vaulter can stall out if he gets over-anxious and attempts to pull on the pole too soon. Another way of looking at it is that the arms are collapsing and not remaining a constant distance from the pole while the pole is unwinding.

ii. Correction

Patience is the key here, as well as the courage to lie back and get the sensation of falling back on the ground. You must make the vaulter acutely conscious that this experience is a part of vaulting or he is going to naturally fight to save himself. There is a tremendous tendency for young vaulters to pull too soon and that is why guarding against it must be constantly emphasized, right from the initial classroom presentation.

4. Improper release from the pole

i. Cause 1

The main cause of a poor release from the pole is the failure to get the pole up to its vertical. There is no way in the world a vaulter can travel the distance from the pole to the bar if the pole is at too great an angle to the bar at release.

ii. Correction

You correct this problem by combatting stalling and you combat stalling, in most cases, by correcting the run, plant and take-off. If this is beginning to sound like a broken record, I am making my point. More than any other event, vaulting is a matter of progression and faults at the end are most often caused by mistakes in the beginning.

i. Cause 2

A second factor that can destroy a good release is the failure of the vaulter to get the hips over the head in the rock-back. If the hips stay out and away from the pole it is invariably going to result in a premature release.

ii. Correction

Go back to the drills previously described for this action. Rope drills, drills with a partner holding the pole or on the football goal post, and, best of all the Butt Burner drill previously described are the best means of working on this problem. Also, it might be advantageous for the coach to assist the pole to its vertical as a temporary measure if the problem becomes serious enough.

i. Cause 3

Releasing with both hands at once at the top of vault often can knock the bar off the standard. It is a shame to lose an otherwise excellent vault with a careless error, but, one that is not uncommon.

ii. Correction

Releasing with both hands at once tends to drop the vaulter straight down. Releasing with the bottom hand first and the top hand last keeps the vaulter in continuous rotation away from the bar. It is a point that can be easily drilled on, just to form the habit. It requires scrutiny, however, because it does happen often.

F. LOCATION OF THE VAULTING STANDARDS

In discussing the correction of common faults among high school vaulters, I have deliberately avoided the issue of standard placement. There is a great temptation to compensate for vaulting faults by moving the standards up or back to take advantage of the location of maximum height. When you do this, you are simply compensating for an athlete's faults and not correcting them. Moving the standards can be a crutch and should be avoided if you want to develop proper technique.

The location of the standards is vitally important, however. The coach and vaulter must determine the best standard location for that particular individual and the vaulter must place the pole in the box before every vault and carefully check to be sure the standards are exactly where he wants them. A vaulter must never take it for granted the standards are right or allow someone else to set them for him. There is absolutely no excuse for blowing a vault because the standards were not right.

There will, of course, be occasions where the movement of the standards in competition can mean the difference between victory and defeat. I would never adjust standards in competition on the basis of one vault. The youngster may just have done something wrong on that particular vault and moving the standards may result in knocking the bar down with a perfect vault. Only if a consistent pattern is developing in a meet should this expediency be considered. In competition you do not want the youngster worrying about standard location, you want him concentrating on good technique. There will be times, however, when adjusting the standards is a good move; just do not do it arbitrarily.

G. COMMITMENT TO THE POLE VAULT

As was said at the outset of this chapter, a school should make a full commitment to the pole vault or should not include it in its track and field program. A good jumping pit that meets all regulations and safety standards, a proper planting box, good jumping standards and a satisfactory runway are all absolute essentials. You must also have a large complement of good poles. There is no question this represents a sizable initial investment and adequate funds are necessary for replacing poles and building a stock pile. It should be re-emphasized that you should never put a youngster on a pole other than one built for his particular weight. The more candidates you have, the more poles you are going to need. There is no way to improvise on this. If you do not have a sufficient stock pile of poles, there is no way you can have an extensive vaulting program. Never gamble with a youngster's safety, or with legal suits against yourself for that matter. It takes a number of years before you can stockpile a decent inventory of poles unless your school is willing to make a very large initial investment. We are in a position now where we budget for three poles a year. This is more than many schools but less than others. We wait until as close to the start of the season as deliveries will allow before deciding on what size poles we will purchase for the year. We call in our most experienced vaulters, check their weights, compare the results with our inventory and make a decision on what size poles we want to order. We always hold off on one pole for which we are budgeted in case we have a pole break during the season and do not have a replacement in stock. If we get lucky and don't break a pole during the season, we simply purchase one at the season's end. We also cultivate good relations with other schools committed to the pole vault in order to make an exchange if possible should we get into a serious bind. The important thing is to protect yourself against broken poles. All high school vaulting coaches live in fear of their top vaulter's breaking his pole just before or in the middle of a key competition with no replacement available. It is imperative to protect yourself as much as possible from this possibility.

Finally, it is advanageous to develop just a little bit of elitism among your pole vaulters. Some coaches may not agree with this, and certainly we want our vaulters to be as conscious of the team concept in track and field as everyone else. The unique nature of the event, however, makes them a little special, almost a team within a team, with their own espirit de corps. Comradery among pole vaulters is essential because they have to work so closely together and depend upon each other. We never allow loafing around when an individual is vaulting. Everyone is assigned either as a spotter or to watch some aspect of the vault to assist the coach in his analysis. Vaulters have to be close and care about each other because they are often called upon to take a pretty good shot from a falling teammate in order to prevent serious injury.

The pole vault is a very difficult event and vaulters should feel special for being involved in it. Of course, we do not want to create a bunch of prima donnas, but that doesn't happen when you demand strict standards from your athletes. The event is unique, however, and we treat it as such. There must be a full commitment from the school administrative authorities, the athletic director, the coach and the athletes if there is any hope of building a successful pole vaulting program.

SAMPLE POLE VAULT WORK WEEK (MID-SEASON)

Monday:

30 Min. Flexibility and warm-up
10 Min. Uniform running
10 Min. Step run throughs

Advanced	Beginners
45 Min. Vaulting 1' below max. height	60 min. Vaulting 1' below max.
15 Min. All out 660 yard run	15 Min. All out 660 yard run
45 Min. Heavy weight workout	

SAMPLE POLE VAULT WORK WEEK (MID-SEASON) (*cont.*)

Tuesday:

30 Min. Flexibility and warm-up

Advanced	Beginners
20 Min. Butt burner drill	10 Min. Pole plant drill
10 Min. Rope drills	10 Min. Step run throughs
15 Min. 5 × 10 yard handwalks	45 Min. Vaulting 6″ below max.
15 Min. 10 × 50 yard relaxed running with pole	45 Min. Heavy weight workout
15 Min. 6 × 220 80% walking in between	

Wednesday:

30 Min. Flexibility and warm-up

Advanced	Beginners
30 Min. Step run-throughs	20 Min. Butt burner drill
45 Min. Vaulting 6″ below max.	10 Min. Rope drills
30 Min. Anaerobic ladder running	15 Min. 5 × 50 yard handwalks
45 Min. Explosive weight workout	15 Min. 5 × 50 yard relaxed running with pole
	15 Min. 10 × downhill running
	30 Min. 6 × 220's 80% walking in between

Thursday:

30 Min. Flexibility and warm-up
10 Min. Step run-throughs

Advanced	Beginners
45 Min. Vaulting 6″ below max.	45 Min. Explosive weight workout
20 Min. 10 × 110's 80% walking in between	20 Min. Pole planting drill
15 Min. 660 yard run 90%	30 Min. Anaerobic ladder running

Friday:

Rest or optional light loosening workout (Advanced)

Goal Day (Beginners)

Saturday:

Competition:
Regular weight workout

CHAPTER 10

COACHING THE SHOT PUT

A. PRESENTING THE EVENT

The first step in teaching any of the throwing events should be a classroom session where the simple basic principles of the event are presented to the prospective candidates. It is essential that the young athletes have a basic understanding of the event if the teaching process is to have any meaning. In the shot put classroom presentation the main purpose is to develop two themes: First, a determination of the factors that make the implement go farther; and second, the concept of sequence or breaking the event down into its four basic stages.

1. What makes the shot travel farther?

It should be impressed upon the young athletes that there are really only two factors that make the shot travel greater distances: (1) the force with which the shot leaves the hand, and (2) the angle of delivery. All technique is designed to enhance one of these two factors. The velocity with which the shot leaves the hand is determined by adding momentum to what amounts to the strongest possible standing delivery or put. This is a concept youngsters can readily understand. The angle of delivery that provides maximum distance is roughly 40 degrees. It is important to impress upon the athletes that putting the shot is much like firing a cannon.

As you raise the elevation of the barrel the shell travels farther until you reach a certain point and then it begins to come back to you. In the artillery it is called high-angle fire and it is the effect one gets when firing from one side of a hill at an enemy on the immediate opposite side. The point that must be impressed, therefore, is that you do not want high-angle fire; height is not the objective. You must seek an angle of delivery of roughly 40 degrees to obtain maximum distance.

2. The sequence or four stages of putting the shot

The four basic stages of shot putting that all young athletes must understand are: (1) the momentum phase, (2) the lift, (3) the delivery, and (4) the follow-through. Each of these four stages must be completed before the next can begin. This will never happen with beginners unless they are thoroughly schooled in the importance of sequence before they ever begin. It is also necessary, however, to emphasize that timing is of vital importance. One stage must blend smoothly and quickly into the next with no stopping in between. It must be impressed upon the youngsters that the shot is in constant motion, first because of the action across the circle, second as the lifting action takes place and finally as it is delivered or put. Any stopping between these stages destroys this constant motion, but, on the other hand, a failure to complete one stage before entering into the next eliminates getting the full body into the throw which is essential for maximum distance. I firmly believe that if a young athlete does not fully understand this concept of sequence and timing, the techniques you try to teach are going to have very little meaning.

a. The follow-through

In all throwing events, the follow-through is not a part of the throw itself, although it does play an extremely vital role in the entire process. Following-through too soon may well be the most common fault for beginners in all three throwing events and because it is so prevalent, a basic understanding of the principles behind the follow-through must be made clear before the athlete begins to develop technique.

i. *Explaining the principles of the follow-through:* The following explanation is used for all three throwing events, and often we bring all three groups together for this part of the classroom presentations. This is all very basic, but my experience has shown that beginners simply have no concept of what the follow-through is all about.

The first thing to impress upon them is that the follow-through takes place after the implement leaves the hand and never before the delivery is completed. If an athlete is right-handed, the throw is always made off the left leg. A left-handed athlete will always throw off the right leg. The interesting thing is that if you put a rock or baseball in a youngster's hand, he or she will follow the above principle pretty well. Put a shot, discus or javelin in the same youngster's hand and inevitably the rear leg will come through as the implement is delivered. To emphasize this point we have each individual take a position as though he or she were about to throw a rock, without being able to move the feet. The right-handers will all stand with the left leg forward and the left-handers just the opposite. We then have them stand with the wrong foot forward and say, "How far do you think you could throw from this position?" The inference is obvious and we point out that this position is actually the one they would be in if they follow-through before the delivery. Again, you must make sure they all understand this and accept it or they are very likely to develop the fault of following through too soon right from the beginning—a fault that becomes increasingly difficult to break.

ii. *Explaining why the follow-through is used:* This explanation always leads to the question, if the follow-through is not part of the throw, then why use it? We answer this question by using the illustration of hitting a baseball. Once contact is made and the ball leaves the bat, there is nothing further we can do to add distance, the latter has already been determined. Why then not stop the swing as soon as the ball leaves the bat? The answer is that if you were swinging the bat at maximum velocity when contact with the ball was made, then stopped abruptly, you would break your arms. The follow-through is necessary simply to give you time to slow the swing down after striking the ball at maximum velocity. The same principle is true in throwing and the analogy of hitting the baseball makes this much easier to understand. It should be impressed upon the athlete that if you throw without following through, you are holding back and not throwing with the full force of the body.

We also stress, of course, that a follow-through is necessary because all throwing events must take place within a legally established limit. The shot and discus are thrown within a circle and the javelin with a restraining line. The follow-through also serves the very vital function of preventing fouling.

The discussion of the follow-through is concluded by emphasizing that as important as it is, if executed too soon, the damage is far greater than if we hold back a bit, so that follow-through is not necessary, and throw off the correct foot. The follow-through is always the last thing we teach and we want them to understand why.

B. TEACHING THE SHOT PUT

1. The throwing position

The first step in teaching shot-putting technique is the throwing position. It is not the purpose of this book to explain things you already know, but to develop methods of coaching those techniques. We teach the throwing position in the gym without an implement. Everything is dependent upon a good start. If you do not begin from the proper position, you cannot expect much to happen correctly after that. Take all the prospective candidates and place them in the proper position step by step. Once we have them fairly well the way we want them, we divide them into partners. On your command one half assume a good throwing position while the partners make corrections and you go around checking. Keep repeating this process until you are satisfied that the athlete can assume the correct position and that the partner rates it satisfactory. The use of the partner system makes a teacher out of each athlete and greatly facilitates the learning process.

It is also good practice to print a step-by-step description of the throwing position and give each candidate a copy. They can go home and practice getting into the proper position in front of a mirror, or with the help of Dad or an older brother.

DESCRIPTION OF SHOT PUT THROWING POSITION
(Given to Shot Put Candidates)

1. Stand in the direction of the throw and then turn so you are facing 90 degrees sideways to the direction of throw.
2. Spread the legs about 36 inches apart. (This will vary with the individual, the great ones, who are probably much bigger than you, take about a 39 inch spread.)
3. Place the toes of both feet on a line through the center of the circle. The line is in the direction of flight. Move the toes of the left foot back 6 inches to the left of the center line. (This will also vary with the individual. Actually the distance should be one half the width of the hips.)
4. Move the right or rear foot 45 degrees away from the direction of flight. This will put the rear foot at an angle of 135 degrees to the direction of flight. (See Figure 10.1.)
5. The weight should be on the ball of the right foot with the left heel up and only the toes of the left foot in contact with the ground for balance.

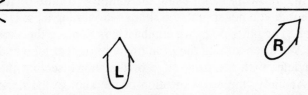

FIGURE 10.1 Position of Feet in Throwing or Putting Position

6. The head and shoulders should be facing directly to the rear with the left arm reaching beyond and slightly below the right knee. The right hand is holding the shot securely in the neck.
7. Both legs should be bent at about a one-quarter squat position. Keep the knees in direct line with the toes.
8. The trunk is erect, the head up and the back straight. Be sure the trunk is directly over the rear leg.

All of the above is for a right-handed putter. (See Figure 10.2.)

2. The grip

In teaching the grip it should be emphasized that you pick up the shot in the left hand (for right-handed throwers) and place it against the

FIGURE 10.2 Throwing or Putting Position

first three fingers of the throwing hand, using the thumb and little finger as guides. Emphasize that you never grab the shot as if palming a basketball but bring it to you. The other point we emphasize is to place the shot securely in the neck. We teach aiming the little finger at the ear lobe and the thumb at the clavicle, with the front edge of the shot bisecting the middle of the chin. Actually, the exact location of the shot in the neck will vary due to physical characteristics. The key is to be sure it is securely in the neck.

3. Punch the mugger

We have an exercise we use at this point that is not original. We picked it up at a coaching clinic, but it represents the best tool for getting across the basic concept of shot-putting I have ever seen. Line up all your candidates facing 90 degrees to your right. Tell them you are an eight-foot mugger coming at them from their left side. When you holler they are to punch the mugger in the nose. Almost naturally you will find them using the proper hip and arm action. After repeating this a few times, ask them to bend their knees before you holler punch the mugger, then lift as you punch getting the legs into it. Youngsters get a great kick out of this drill and what they are doing, quite naturally, is simulating the action you are looking for in the shot. Try it, it is a lot of fun and it works.

4. Teaching the lift

The previous drill is a good start for teaching the lift stage which, in reality, is a lift and simultaneous lead with the hip. Actually, you want three movements all at once—a vigorous lifting action with the rear leg, the head raising so the eyes are looking straight up in the air, and the hips rotating to the front. Have the athletes get into a standing position without the shot, and on your command "lift" have them execute the three movements simultaneously and stop there so you can check them out. Don't say anything about the left leg at first. Hopefully, this action will result in the left foot pointing in the direction of flight and the left heel coming down almost to the ground. If this doesn't happen by itself, then you must add it to your instruction. The lifting action of the left leg, which comes next, cannot take place properly if the left foot is not in the correct position. If you can accomplish this, however, without the youngsters thinking about it, you are that much better off. Once they have this concept down, add the lifting action of the left leg as soon as the heel comes down, still without the shot in the athlete's hand. When complete, it should all happen in one quick motion.

5. Drills for teaching the lift

Once your athletes have the idea of lifting and rotating the hips without the shot, there are two good drills to use to teach the lifting action with the implement. First, have them assume a good throwing position and place the shot, held in place with both hands, directly on the groin area. Tell them to put the shot using only the legs and hip, being sure to keep the trunk erect and not bend backward. The shot can be propelled a few feet this way, but only with the proper lifting action.

A second drill is to have them assume a proper throwing position, with the shot properly in the neck, lined up under the limb of a tree that is about three to four feet in front of the athletes, almost directly overhead. Have them put the shot and hit the limb. Again, the only way this can be done is by the proper lifting action. The idea is to get them to feel what the lifting action is like and then transfer it into the actual putting process.

6. Teaching the delivery

In teaching the delivery, go back again to the punch-the-mugger drill, but now tell the youngsters to point the thumb downward when delivering the punch. We do this a few times and then explain that the delivery of the shot is nothing more than a push-up action, completed by an outward snapping of the wrist, with the thumb pointed downward. Have them stand erect, facing the line of flight, in the exact position you want the body to be in at the moment of release, and, without the shot, execute this action. (See Figures 10.3 and 10.4.)

You really cannot work on delivery without the lifting action. Before combining, however, you must emphasize the fact that there are two distinct stages and that the vigorous action of the right shoulder first, and then the right arm, does not start until the lifting action is complete. In other words, tell them the shot has been moving because you have been lifting it, and, since it can no longer move any further in that manner and it be kept in motion, now you must deliver with the right shoulder and arm. This naturally has to be all in one quick motion and we constantly emphasize–lift and put.

7. Drills for teaching delivery

A good method for getting the athletes to deliver in a proper erect position is to have them do standing puts from behind a waist-high fence. A waist-high jumping pit can serve the same purpose. Put the athletes right up to the fence as though it were a toe board and have them put

FIGURE 10.3   Delivery Position as Arm Action Begins

without a follow-through. This really promotes proper body positioning in the delivery.

A second drill involves using an indoor shot and throwing at a target marked on a wall. This has to be done on an individual basis to allow for differences in ability. You determine the distance each putter should stand from the wall, and then mark a target on the wall that represents the 40-degree angle of delivery you are seeking. You could do this just as well aiming at or over a fence or at a target suspended on a rope tied between two jumping standards or poles. The big key on this, however, is to set the target and throwing location accurately for each individual.

8. Adding the follow-through

We do not add the follow-through to the process until we feel the athlete has been well ingrained with delivering properly over the front

FIGURE 10.4   Body Position at Release

leg. It is rather simple to teach an accomplished putter to get more out over the board and then vigorously replace the left or front leg with the right. It is extremely difficult to break someone who reverses prematurely, and that is inevitably what you are going to get if you teach the reverse too soon.

9. Teaching the action across the circle

It is very important not to spend too much of your time with the standing put and to be sure to emphasize the action across the circle. The standing put technique should be taught first, but it is essential to begin to teach the action across the circle separately by the end of the first week of instruction. In theory, all the action across the circle accomplishes is to add momentum to a good standing put. The reality, however, is not that simple as it is quite difficult to transfer from the action across the circle to the lift. I am convinced that at least half of the throwing portion of each workout should be spent working across the circle. We mimeograph the steps of the action as we do the throwing position so that youngsters can take the instructions home and work on the technique on their own. We also use the same partner system as we do in teaching the standing put; having the partners check each other and criticize each other's technique. All of this is done without a shot. Once they can get across the circle into a good throwing position without the shot, then introduce the implement and start throwing with the full action. As soon as you put a shot in the hands of most beginners they appear to forget everything you have taught them. The process of combining the action across the circle with the actual lifting and putting action takes a lot of patience. I am convinced, however, that you cannot expect an athlete to execute this technique properly with the shot if he cannot first accomplish it correctly without it.

DESCRIPTION OF THE SHOT PUT ACTION ACROSS THE CIRCLE:
(Given to Shot Put candidates)

1. Stand erect with the right foot forward facing the rear of the circle. Hold the left hand high and in line with the shot. Tuck the shot securely in the neck with the elbow down.
2. Bend forward so the trunk is parallel to the ground, the eyes are up and the shot is well outside the circle.
3. Raise the left leg so the body forms a "T" position. (See Figure 10.5.)
4. Bring the left knee in to a position near the right knee in what is called an "A" position. (See Figure 10.6.)
5. Vigorously drive across the circle with the left foot shooting out front in a scissors-like action. Keep the head and shoulders facing the rear. Reach beyond and below the right knee with the left hand.
6. Think of snapping across the circle. Stay as close to the ground as you can without causing friction and thereby slowing down. Come across the circle so that the rear foot lands directly in the center of it. (The distance across the circle will vary for each individual. The ideal is to land in your best throwing or standing put position with the left toe just barely touching the toe board.) The right foot should land simultaneously with (or even slightly before) the left foot's contact with the ground.

FIGURE 10.5   T-Position

7. Land in a good standing put or throwing position. Be sure the weight is well over the rear leg. (The action just described is therefore: Up - down - T - A - Snap into the throwing or standing put position.)
8. Initiate the lifting action as soon as the left toe makes contact with the ground.

FIGURE 10.6   A-Position

C. TRAINING THE HIGH SCHOOL
SHOT-PUTTER

The training program for high school shot-putters should be divided fairly evenly between running, quickness and agility work; strength training; and technique work.

1. Running workouts

We devote roughly 30 minutes each day to this type of training. Our sprint work for shot-putters involves a lot of 10-yard races for quickness, uphill and downhill running just as we give our sprinters, football agility drills and timed 40-yard dashes. Since so many of our shot-putters are also football players we kill two birds with one stone here, but we do not do this for football as it is just as necessary to work on these areas in the weight events. Finally, we do a lot of one-legged hopping up the stadium stairs to develop both balance and strength on one leg. If you analyze shot-putting technique, it is apparent how much of the action is actually performed with the weight and balance over one leg. We feel the one-legged hopping drills, on each leg, are an absolute must for the shot-putter.

2. Strength training

Shot-putting is essentially a weight lifting event. Although we have never done this simply because we cannot get control of the youngsters soon enough, I honestly believe that if an athlete was involved in an intense weight training program for two full years before you even introduced the shot to that individual, the learning process would be much easier. You simply cannot perform the techniques required in this event (unless you perform them without the shot) without considerable strength.

You will never have an athlete as strong as you would like him to be, and most will never really be strong enough for successful shot-putting. You must, however, work with what you have and develop as much strength as possible. You can gain a measure of success in any other event in track and field without weight training, although I certainly don't recommend such a course, but not in the shot put. If your shot-putters are not dedicated year-round weight lifters, they are wasting their time if real success in the event is their ultimate goal.

In the off-season our shot-putters lift three times a week alternating heavy and regular workouts as described in Chapter 2. Once into the competitive season a three-workouts-per-week program is utilized, consisting of a heavy - regular - explosive sequence, never lifting the day before competition and with the explosive workout always preceding major competition. This program should be flexible, however, for each individual. Many beginners, for instance, might be well advised to continue the off-season schedule right through the competitive season. Certain individuals with great strength and poor quickness could well benefit during the heart of the competitive season from a regular - explosive - explosive schedule. It is the role of the coach to work out a program designed to meet each individual's needs.

Free Weight Program	Weight Machine Program
Bench press	Bench press
Behind neck military press	Military press
Inclined press	Inclined press
Squats	Front trunk twists
Heel raises	Forearm curls
Clean and jerk	Upright rowing
Forearm curls	Dips
Upright rowing	Leg press
Inclined sit-ups	Inclined sit-ups
Leg lifts	Leg lifts
Leg extensions	Kneeling alternating
Leg curls	pulldowns
	Leg extensions
	Leg curls

3. Technique training

It never should be assumed that once learned never forgotten. Do not hesitate to go back to any of the drills used in teaching the event, especially when you see faults developing. Even with our best athletes we like to begin each throwing workout with the three drills previously described—the throws at the tree limb, throwing behind the waist-high fence and standing throws at a target. We alternate days, throwing and weight training, with 30 minutes of running every day. We throw for roughly an hour, devoting the first half of the workout to the drills and standing puts and the second half to putting with the action across the circle. As has been said before, it is a mistake to spend too much time on the standing put seeking perfection because you are never going to attain it. Further, the lifting action is extremely difficult to accomplish while going across the circle and you are never going to get it unless you spend a great deal of time working on it. You compete with the action across the circle, not from a standing put, and you must practice what you are going to do in competition.

Working across the circle, I like to use three athletes to assist me while one of their colleagues is putting. I have one watch where the left foot lands as the action is completed across the circle and the athlete lands in the throwing position. The second assistant watches where the right foot lands at the same stage, while the third checks to be sure the head, shoulders and left arm are all well to the rear as the throwing position is attained. I will watch whatever we are working on for that particular throw. A coach can never watch effectively more than one thing at a time, just as the athlete cannot concentrate on more than one aspect of the technique. The reason for having the three partners watch the three points mentioned is that if the youngster is not landing in the correct position, other faults will come about as a result. In attempting to correct faults, always go back to the core first. Also, concentrate on the most consistent faults, don't try to point out every thing that is wrong on every throw.

4. The use of visual aids

The shot, just as in all other events, can be learned far more effectively with the use of visual aids. We like to show loop films of the greats in action, initially in the classroom presentation and periodically throughout the training process. We also try to utilize videotaping or filming of the athletes performing their events as well as still shots at various stages of the putting action. We often bring the books and the pictures right out on the field during practice. In all events, there is no substitute for the athlete's seeing how the event should be performed correctly and for analyzing visually one's own technique.

D. ANALYZING THE MOST COMMON FAULTS FOUND IN HIGH SCHOOL SHOT-PUTTERS

1. Opening up coming across the circle

Opening up means moving the head and shoulders in the direction of flight before landing in a proper throwing position.

i. Cause

Opening up invariably is a result of over-anxiousness, or over-emphasis of the left arm action. It results in a premature shifting of the weight and a consequent loss of the legs in the lift and putting phases.

ii. Correction

The key to preventing an opening up action is to stress keeping the head and shoulders to the rear when coming across the circle, with the left arm reaching beyond and below the right knee. At the high school level I am convinced it is a mistake to teach the proper left arm action too soon in the learning process. If you study films of the great shot putters, you will see the left arm begins its wide sweeping arc before the left toe makes contact with the ground and the athlete lands in a proper throwing position. The left arm actually leads the lifting and rotation of the hips, but the head and shoulders are still to the rear when the left toe makes contact with the ground. I feel that if you stress this action too soon, your athletes will open up too quickly. Just tell them to swing the left arm high and wide as they lift. You can add the refinement of proper timing of the left arm when you have an accomplished putter. In the beginning, don't do anything that hinders landing in a proper throwing position.

2. Starting the putting action too soon

This may actually happen as the athlete comes across the circle, or just as he or she reaches the throwing position. Either way it eliminates the lifting stage and this is what separates the great putters from the mediocre.

i. Cause

Again, this is usually a case of over-anxiousness. It is also a product of the very natural desire to propel the body in the direction of flight of the implement, rather than into an erect position.

ii. Correction

It is necessary to continually emphasize delaying the putting action until the lift is completed. A thorough knowledge and acceptance of the sequence concept by the athlete is an absolute necessity to prevent premature putting and this is why it is stressed right from the initial classroom presentation. Constant repetition of the lifting drills previously described, particularly the putting at the tree limb drill, can be very helpful in correcting this problem.

3. Premature movement of the head in the direction of flight

This may begin during the action across the circle but more likely will take place as the lifting stage begins.

i. Cause

Premature looking in the direction of flight is caused by a natural desire to see where the shot is going. It is extremely serious because it again results in a premature shifting of the weight and subsequent loss of the legs in the lift and put.

ii. Correction

Putting the shot blindfolded is a very effective method of curing a youngster's natural desire to see where it is going. Also, extensive stress on proper head positioning in each stage of the put is imperative: (1) to the rear as you come across the circle into the throwing position, (2) straight up in the air during the lifting action, (3) out in the direction of flight as you deliver, (4) off to the left (right-handed putter) as you reverse.

4. Dropping the elbow during delivery

i. Cause

This is caused by the natural tendency to want to throw the shot rather than put it.

ii. Correction

The key to prevent dropping the elbow is to emphasize keeping the thumb down and snapping the wrist outward. Stress that the proper putting action is similar to doing a push-up. The desire to put too soon also will lead to dropping of the elbow.

5. Reversing too soon

i. Cause

Once more, this fault is caused by over-anxiousness and a failure to fully understand and accept the sequence concept. Athletes who reverse too soon either do not understand the proper delivery position off the front foot or are trying to do everything at once.

ii. Correction

The secret of preventing premature reversing is not to teach the action too soon. Make sure the athlete can deliver properly before introducing the reverse. Putting from the waist-high fence without using the reverse is also a very helpful tool in curing this fault.

E. SPECIAL PROBLEMS IN COACHING
GIRL SHOT-PUTTERS

As in all field events, there is no boys' technique vs. girls' technique in shot-putting. The special problem in shot-putting for girls lies in their upper body and leg strength. There is no event in track and field where the gap in strength between girls and boys is as much a factor as in shot-putting. In theory, since the girls' shot weighs roughly two-thirds of the boys' shot, the girls ought to be able to handle two-thirds of what the boys can handle in the weight room. This, of course, does not even come close to being the case. Further, you are going to have a very rough time with Mommy and Daddy if you try to turn daughter into a dedicated weight lifter as you should be doing with your male shot-putters. We insist all our girls work on the weights and have outlined our program previously, but any intensification of weight training must be the decision of the young lady herself.

Because girls lack sufficient upper body and leg strength, it is entirely possible that some of your girls are not going to be able to master the O'Brien style of shot putting. We teach this style first just as we do with the boys, but if we see a girl who just cannot handle it, we will try the old-fashioned facing the side style. Although this method is not as productive as the O'Brien style it produced some very fine distances in the old days. It does not require the same degree of balance and leg strength as the O'Brien and may produce much better results for many girls. Let's be practical, most of your girl shot-putters are never going to go near a shot again after they leave high school. Use for the girls the style that gets the best results. With some we have even used a one-two-three walking action or a hopping action across the circle just to get a little momentum. In many cases the O'Brien style may not be the most productive method of shot-putting at the high school level, particularly for the girls.

SAMPLE SHOT PUT WORK WEEK (MID-SEASON)

Monday:

30 min. flexibility and warm-up
30 min. Shot put drills (Fence, Tree limb, Standing puts at target)

SAMPLE SHOT PUT WORK WEEK (MID-SEASON) (*cont.*)

60 min. Heavy weight workout
15 min. 6 × 110's 80% walking in between
15 min. 3 × 220's 80% walking in between

Tuesday:

30 min. Flexibility and warm-up
30 min. Shot put drills
10 min. Circle work—no shot
30 min. Throwing through circle
15 min. 10 × 10 yard races
15 min. Stair hopping drills

Wednesday:

30 min. Flexibility and warm-up
60 min. Explosive weight workout
15 min. 10 × downhill running
15 min. 10 × uphill running
30 min. Shot Put drills

Thursday:

30 min. Flexibility and warm-up
15 min. Standing puts
15 min. Circle work—no shot
30 min. Throwing through circle
15 min. 2 × 40 yard dashes timed
15 min. 3 × Whistlers (relaxation sprinting)

Friday:

Rest or optional light loosening workout (Advanced)

Goal Day (Beginners)

Regular weight workout (Beginners)

Saturday:

Competition

Regular weight workout (Advanced)—after competition

CHAPTER 11

COACHING THE DISCUS

A. PRESENTING THE EVENT

As in all field events we introduce the discus event to all prospective candidates in a classroom session. It is a good idea to begin the presentation with some loop films of the greats in action in order to allow the beginners the opportunity to see what the event looks like when performed correctly. As we do with the shot put, we emphasize the two major factors that make any implement go farther: (1) the force with which the discus leaves the hand, and (2) the angle of delivery, roughly 35–40 degrees. We use the same basic artillery analogy as explained in the chapter on shot-putting to illustrate the concept of delivery angle.

In the case of the discus, however, we must also explain a third major factor—aerodynamics. As far as the athlete is concerned this really involves only two factors: (1) getting a good rotation of the implement to insure stability, and (2) keeping the nose of the discus down to prevent it from stalling out. There are a tremendous amount of highly technical factors involved in discus throwing, as is true in many events, and, as important as they may be, you can easily confuse the athlete with too much information. It makes no sense to fill the youngster's head with a lot of scientific data that can be counter-productive. All the athlete needs to know is the basic principle of the event—keep your explanation clear and simple.

In the discus, the classroom presentation should also be directed at promoting an understanding of the four basic stages of the discus throw: (1) momentum or the action across the circle, (2) leading with the hip, (3) the delivery, and (4) the follow-through. We explain carefully to our discus throwers the concept of sequence and the importance of completing each stage of the execution of the event before the next can begin. They must be made to understand that they can not become over-anxious and overlap the phases, but they must also understand the vital importance of proper timing. It is essential to point out that there must be no stopping between stages and each stage must blend smoothly and quickly into the next.

Finally, we explain the role of the follow-through, emphasizing the fact it takes place after and not before the discus leaves the hand. We use the same approach to explaining the follow-through in the discus that we used in the shot. In fact, we often bring the candidates for all three throwing events together for this presentation. This explanation is described in detail in the chapter on shot-putting and will not be repeated here. Refer to the shot put chapter if you are not familiar with this explanation.

B. TEACHING THE DISCUS THROW

1. The grip and release

The first things we work on, following the initial classroom presentation, are the the grip and release. We teach the grip by asking the athlete to take his or her thumb and bisect the discus so that the fingers are pointing off at an angle to the right (right-handed throwers). Tell them to move the whole hand leftward until the first digits of the fingers grip the edge of the discus with the fingers spread at medium width. We then instruct them to hold the discus with the palm down maintaining pressure on the discus with the thumb. At this point we have them flip the discus out about 30 feet or so, instructing them to think of ripping the discus in half so that it rotates in flight in a clockwise fashion. We scatter our prospects all over the field in pairs, being sure each pair is a safe distance from other throwers, and tell them to keep flipping the discus back and forth to each other in this manner, making sure the disc is coming off the first finger and is rotating clockwise with the nose of the discus down. It should be emphasized that it is necessary to eliminate those aerodynamic factors that hinder flight before we can move on to other aspects of the technique. This is a point that was emphasized strongly in the classroom presentation. Most experts say the ideal angle of incidence is from 5–10 degrees with allowances having to be made for wind conditions. We just tell our prospects—"Keep the nose down."

2. The throwing position

Once we feel our candidates have the idea of the proper release, we teach the throwing position. Just as in the shot, we mimeograph directions for assuming a correct throwing position so they can take it home and work on the position in front of a mirror. Care should be taken to prepare a separate sheet for left-handed throwers so that they will be spared the confusion of having to transpose. In teaching the throwing position take the candidates through the process step by step until they can assume a relatively correct stance. Then, break the candidates into partners and on your command one partner assumes the throwing position while the other makes corrections. The coach goes around constantly checking, repeating the process over and over until everybody can set himself in a good position without the need of correcting.

DESCRIPTION OF DISCUS STANDING THROW POSITION
(Given to discus candidates)

1. Stand in the direction of the throw and then turn so you are facing 90 degrees sideways to the direction of throw.
2. Spread the legs about 36 inches apart. (This will vary slightly with each individual, depending on your size.)
3. Place the toes of both feet on a line through the center of the circle. The line is in the direction of flight. Move the toes of the left foot back 6 inches to the left of the center line. (This will also vary with each individual.) Actually the distance should be one-half the width of the hips.
4. Move the right foot or rear foot 45 degrees farther away from the direction of flight. This will put the rear foot at an angle of 135 degrees to the direction of flight.

5. The weight should be on the ball of the right foot with the left heel up and only the toes of the left foot in contact with the ground for balance.
6. The head and shoulders should be facing directly to the rear with the left arm curled across the chest. The discus is held well back in the right hand.
7. Both legs are bent in about a one-quarter squat position. Keep the knees in direct line with the toes.
8. The trunk is erect, the head is up and the back straight. Be sure the trunk is directly over the rear leg.

All of the above is for a right-handed thrower.

3. The standing throw

Once the youngster has mastered a decent release and can assume a proper throwing position, we begin to teach the standing throw. The discus is a little different from the shot at this stage. In the shot you teach lift and rotation of the hips simultaneously; in the discus you want the rotation of the hips to precede the lifting action.

i. Drills for teaching the hip rotation

In the discus we teach: around - up and out. The first step is to have the athletes assume the throwing position without a discus and on the command "rotate," rotate the hips and lift with the legs, holding it at that point with the throwing arm still well back so you can check it out. Again, as in the shot, we do not say anything about the left foot. Hopefully, it will rotate to the front with the heel coming down and then raise up again as the lift with the left leg takes place. If it doesn't happen this way you must add this action into your instruction. We hope this left foot action will happen naturally as we want to keep the thinking process to a minimum. If you can get away without bringing this point out, it is to your advantage, but if you cannot, it must be taught as the action is essential.

An excellent drill to teach this action is to bring your discus throwers into the gym and give each of them a small hoop used by physical education classes that is similar to the old hula hoop. Have them assume the throwing position and throw the hoop as they would the discus without worrying about the release. The idea of leading with the hip, so vital to successful discus throwing, comes across almost naturally throwing these hoops.

ii. The delivery

When you feel they have the idea of leading with the hip, move into the full standing throw. If there are a large number of candidates, you can throw five or six at a time if you use a road bordering on an open field as your throwing area. If you have to go one at a time from the regular discus circle with large numbers, you will not get much throwing in. If this method is used, be sure to have all throwing done on your command and allow no one to retrieve a disc until you give the word, and retrieve all at once. It is also effective to work on standing throws into a fence. This saves a lot of time chasing the implements and also eliminates worrying about how far they are going rather than proper technique.

Once they get into the standing throws, beginners often start forgetting about the release. Keep going back to the release when working on the standing throw. If an athlete begins to lose the good release, have him roll the discus on its edge along a straight line or have him toss it straight up in the air. You must release properly off the first finger to perform either of these drills.

In teaching the delivery, major emphasis must be placed upon delaying the discus as long as possible. It is an easy matter to do this with the hoops or with the discus taped to the hand; it is an entirely different matter when actually throwing. Continually emphasize that the thrower must be in control, and never let the discus control him. Try to get the yongster to the point where he or she can throw the discus in any direction desired. This can never be done without properly leading the hip and delaying the discus. Do not get technical about delivery angle. Ideally you are looking for an angle of flight of about 35–40 degrees. We simply tell the athletes to start the throw from the hips and release at shoulder level. As the discus starts to come around it should be at hip level and when it leaves the hand it should be level with the shoulders. This seems to make more sense to a young athlete when you are dealing with two angles in discus throwing—the angle of flight and the angle of incidence. We try not to confuse the youngsters and merely emphasize throwing from the hips to the shoulders with the nose of the implement down. (See Figures 11.1 and 11.2.)

It is also vital to emphasize keeping the discus as far away from the body as possible in the delivery. This increases the leverage of the throw and also makes it easier to keep the palm down and thereby gain the proper angle of incidence. In order to establish a good erect delivery position with the shoulder square to the direction of flight, we keep telling the youngsters to grow tall when they release and focus the eyes on a distant point in the direct line of flight.

FIGURE 11.1   Delivery from Hip

4. The reverse

As in the shot, do not teach the reverse in the discus until you are satisfied the athlete is throwing properly off the front leg. If you introduce the reverse too soon in the learning process, it becomes extremely likely the rear leg will be brought through too early and the benefit of the legs is lost in the throw. As was said regarding this point in the shot, it is quite simple to teach a vigorous replacement of the front leg with the rear after the discus is released when an athlete delivers properly. It is very difficult to break the habit of reversing too soon.

5. Winding up for the standing throw

Although there may be some merit to the argument that allowing a youngster to wind up in a standing throw helps to transfer hip rotation and lift from the action across the circle, we still do not allow it. Winding up may give a little more distance to the standing throw and may also be a little more comfortable. The trouble is that this is an action that is not

FIGURE 11.2 Delivery at Shoulders

going to take place in the full across-the-circle throw. You do not wind up as you land in a throwing position from the action across the circle. If you let the athletes wind up for a standing throw they are only going to develop bad habits.

6. Teaching the action across the circle

We use the full three-quarter turn, starting facing directly to the rear. The teaching process is begun by having the athletes walk through the circle action by the numbers without a discus: (1) the pivot on the left foot (right-handers) holding the right leg and right arm back, (2) step to the center of the circle with the right foot, holding the right arm low and close to the hip, (3) pivot from there into a correct throwing position. (See Figures 11.3, 11.4 and 11.5.)

Once we have taught the action-across-the-circle step by step by the numbers, we speed the process up and have the athletes jog through the

FIGURE 11.3   Across-Circle Start

FIGURE 11.4   Action Across Circle

FIGURE 11.5   Start of Throwing Action

three-step process just described, ending up in a correct throwing position. Keep on speeding up the action always emphasizing the athlete is running through the circle, not spinning like a top. The discus must always be well back, motionless, and the throwing arm completely relaxed.

When the youngster can execute the action across the circle properly without a discus, then tape one to the hand and repeat the process. Again, gradually speed up the action until a speed is reached you feel the youngster can handle. Always emphasize that speed across the circle is great provided it can be handled. What this means is that the athlete must land in a proper throwing position. If this does not happen, the athlete is not in control and going too fast.

While you are devoting part of the practice time to teaching the proper action across the circle, you should also be devoting practice time separately to teaching the standing throw. It is a major mistake to let athletes throw through the circle before they can throw decently from a stand, and execute the action across the circle properly without the discus. On the other hand, don't wait until you have a decent standing throw before you introduce the action across the circle. I believe in teaching the two phases in separate segments of the same practice sessions. We introduce the full across-the-circle throw only when a youngster has mastered a decent standing throw and can combine the entire process reasonably well with the discus taped to the hand.

C. TRAINING THE HIGH SCHOOL DISCUS THROWERS

1. Technique training

A cardinal rule in coaching all events in track and field is never to assume, "Once learned, never forgotten." It is important to go back through the stages of the learning process to periodically re-emphasize the various factors in discus throwing. Even with experienced throwers it makes sense to go back to the steps taken in the teaching process when flagrant faults develop. Utilization of videotape, still shots and films is very valuable in analyzing faults in discus technique. It is imperative also that the coach not fill the athlete's head with too much to think about. It is very tempting to say to a youngster, for example, "Delay the right leg at the start, keep the discus back, lead with the hip, keep the discus away from the body, and the palm down during the delivery." The trouble is that even though he or she must do all these things, there is no way in the world any individual can think about them all at the same time. Be sure to have the athlete concentrate on just one aspect of the technique on each throw, and you do the same. There is a great temptation to over coach in the discus. Do not fall victim to it.

It is very important in coaching technique to give particular attention to the initial stages of the discus action. It is a linear and not a rotation event, but that is a difficult concept to convey because there is, of course, a revolving action that takes place when going across the circle. This lends itself to fault progression. By that I mean, since control is such a vital factor, an error made at the beginning of the process compounds itself and causes other errors as the action progresses. Be very careful to correct the cause and not the result. In all events in track and field, if you do not get started properly you are in trouble, but the discus and the pole vault seem to be the most susceptible to this problem.

The discus is a very dangerous event. It is even more difficult to control than the javelin and should never be thrown with the full circle action without a proper screen around the circle area. Schools that throw the discus without a screen are seriously endangering the athletes and are sticking their necks out for a law suit. When you are in the circle it is strictly a one-at-a-time situation, and this slows the practice down considerably. In the course of a normal workout, discus throwers get far fewer throws than their shot or javelin counterparts, unless you are taking unwarranted risks. For this reason it is important to organize your practice so that no more than five or six throwers are using the discus circle at any one time. If you have large groups of discus throwers, divide them up into ability groups and rotate them. One group, for example could be working in the circle, a second in a vacant field working on release drills, a third in the gym or on a hard top area drilling with the discus taped to their hands, while a fourth group, if you have that many, could be running or working on the weights. The important thing is to split your discus thowers into small groups keeping everyone busy and not creating a jam in the throwing circle.

We spend more time on the circle action in the discus than we do in the shot. We try to achieve a ratio of one-third drills and standing throws to two-thirds work across the circle for our top throwers. Because of circle limitations just the reverse might be true for the less advanced. In working across the circle I assign four athletes to help in analyzing a particular thrower. The first is assigned to watch the right leg (right-handers) at the back of the circle to be sure it does not start around until the weight is firmly distributed over the left or pivoting foot. A second watches the discus throughout the entire action across the circle to be sure it is held well back and relaxed. A third checks the position of the head and shoulders when the thrower lands in the throwing position to be sure they are to the rear. The fourth watches the positioning of the feet as the thrower lands in the throwing position. There is, of course, nothing sacred about using four helpers to watch segments of the action, nor do you have to assign exactly the areas here indicated. You can have as many as you want watch whatever you want. The concept of utilizing team members to assist you in analyzing a thrower is extremely helpful to you as a coach, and is also beneficial as a teaching device for the athletes, while keeping everyone involved in the practice.

I do not feel throwing day after day is as detrimental in the discus as in the shot, although obviously you must guard against too much throwing in any event. Technique is more of a factor in the discus than the shot and we like to devote at least 30 minutes of a practice to technique work. I don't like to let a practice day go by without some technique work. If we feel a younstger has had too much throwing, we can work on drills or with the discus taped to the hand.

2. Strength work

Strength is not the factor in the discus that it is in the shot. It is vital, however, and you should work on it just as hard. The fact that smaller athletes or tall rangy ones who lack beef for the shot are often successful in the discus does not preclude the fact that the stronger they are the better they are going to be. We use the same basic program for discus throwers that we do for shot putters, utilizing the free weights with the boys and the weight machine with the girls. Often we get discus throwers coming to us from other sports who are already into the nautilus or the weight machine. We allow these individuals to continue in their previous programs, making sure that exercises we require for the discus are added if necessary. We prefer free weights for our male discus throwers but we do not force them as long as they are in a constructive program.

Our discus throwers lift three days a week in the off-season,

Free Weight Program	Weight Machine Program
Bench press	Bench press
Military press	Military press
Lateral raise	Front trunk twists
Squats	Forearm curls
Heel raises	Upright rowing
Clean and jerk	Lateral raise
Forearm curls	Kneeling pulldowns
Upright rowing	Dips
Inclined sit-ups	Leg press
Leg lifts	Inclined sit-ups
Leg extensions	Leg lifts
Leg curls	Leg extensions
	Leg curls

alternating heavy and regular workouts the same as do our shot-putters. During the competitive season we again go to the heavy-regular-explosive sequence as in the shot, making sure the explosive workout precedes competition and never lifting on the day prior to a meet. As in the shot, flexibility is vitally important and gearing an individual's program to that particular youngster's needs is essential. But since speed, quickness, agility, etc. play a greater relative role than strength in the discus, we are more inclined to move to a regular - regular - explosive sequence with our discus throwers. In certain cases you might also find it beneficial to limit a discus thrower to just two weight workouts a week when in the heart of the competitive season.

3. Running workouts

We give our discus throwers the same spring and agility work we give our shot-putters. We emphasize 10-yard races, 40-yard dashes for time, uphill running, downhill running, one-legged stairs hopping, rope skipping and football agility drills. We always devote 30 minutes of every practice to this type of activity.

D. ANALYZING THE MOST COMMON FAULTS
IN HIGH SCHOOL DISCUS THROWERS

1. Starting the right leg too soon from the rear of the circle

Failure to delay the right leg until the weight is well distributed over the left or pivoting foot will result in the athlete's being out of control. If this mistake is made, errors will compound from this point on. You absolutely have to get started correctly.

i. Cause

More than anything else, this fault is caused by over-anxiousness to get started or possibly from not being fully aware of the importance of delaying the right leg.

ii. Correction

Have the athlete pivot on the left foot and stop at that point without a discus. Keep on repeating that initial action until it becomes a habit. Also, working through the entire action in the circle with a discus taped to the hand is very helpful in dealing with the problem. You can develop the proper delaying habit by eliminating the distraction of an actual throw, recognizing that what is developed with the discus taped must transfer when the tape is removed.

2. Moving the discus as action across the circle takes place

If the discus is not held motionless and well back throughout the action across the circle, the athlete will also lose control and will have nothing left to throw with when he or she lands in the center of the circle.

i. Cause

This is most often caused by a desire to spin with the discus rather than to hold it back and run through the circle. It is also the result of over-anxiousness to begin the throw.

ii. Correction

Too much winding up is often a factor in this error. We limit our throwers to a maximum of two windups. The windup serves no useful purpose except to get the athlete loose and fluid. Excessive winding up gets the discus moving and that is exactly what you do not want. Also, emphasize that the thrower must think landing in a throwing position and not start the hip rotation until the left toe makes contact with the circle. There is a tremendous tendency to be over-anxious in this phase. You must impress upon the athlete the need to relax, take it easy across the circle and not to attempt to generate speed that cannot be controlled. Again, working with the discus taped to the hand can be very beneficial in dealing with this problem.

3. The flight of the discus goes off to the right (right-handers)

i. Cause

There are two main causes of a flight off to the right. First, the foot placement when landing in the throwing position may not be correct. If the left foot comes down too soon and does not land one-half the width of the hips to the left of the center line, the athlete will throw in the direction the feet are pointing. Second, the athlete may be starting the discus delivery at the same time the hips are beginning to rotate. This will lead to a loss of control, with the discus going off to the right.

ii. Correction

Mark the spots on the circle where you want the feet to land as the athlete completes the action across the circle and lands in the throwing position. Emphasize not being in a hurry to get the left foot down on the ground. The left foot's coming down to the right of where you want is the result of being in a hurry to get into the throwing position. Work on the action across the circle without a discus or with the discus taped to the hand. If the discus delivery is beginning before the hip rotation starts, it could well be because the athlete is not holding the discus well back and is rushing the action across the circle. There is no way a youngster can lead with the hip if he or she does not land in a proper throwing position.

4. The discus hooking off to the left

i. Cause

Again, there are two major causes of this fault. First, it could be again a matter of improper foot placement when landing in the throwing position. If the left foot comes down to the left of one-half the width of the hips to the left of the center line position, the throw will go off to the left minus the power generated by the legs in the proper position. Second, a throw off to the left can be caused by dropping of the left shoulder or turning the left shoulder and arm too far to the left.

ii. Correction

The left foot's coming down too far to the left is almost always the result of not keeping the head and shoulders back when landing in the throwing position. If the head and shoulders start too soon, the hip, and consequently the discus, will also come around too far. Constant emphasis upon holding back, relaxing and not trying to start the throw too soon is the key to avoiding being off to the left. Having the athlete concentrate on keeping the head to the rear when landing in the throwing position, looking straight up as the hip rotation and lift take place, then focusing on a point in the direct line of flight when delivering will correct pulling around to the left. The head is the key to controlling the rest of the body.

5. The discus stalling out

Stalling is a very common problem, especially for beginners, and is the result of the nose of the discus sailing out at too high an angle.

i. Cause

The cause of too high a nose angle and consequent stalling out of the discus is a thrower's failure to keep the palm down during delivery.

ii. Correction

The main point to emphasize upon the athlete who is having difficulty keeping the nose of the discus down is to press down on the discus with the thumb. If you press down with the thumb the palm will stay down. Also, it is very important not to scoop the discus close to the body when executing the delivery. The farther out from the body the discus is held in delivery, the easier it is to keep the palm down and obtain the proper nose angle. In addition, the farther out from the body, the greater the leverage of the throw.

6. Reversing too soon

i. Cause

Like so many other faults in the throwing events, reversing too soon is the result of being over-anxious and bringing everything into play at once rather than in sequence.

ii. Correction

Emphasize hip, right arm, right leg in that order—not all at the same time. Also, hold off teaching the reverse until the abilty to throw off the front leg is well established. With outstanding throwers it is very difficult to determine with the naked eye if the reverse is coming too soon. Check all athletes carefully with film or still shots to be sure the rear leg is not coming through too quickly.

E. SPECIAL PROBLEMS IN COACHING GIRL DISCUS THROWERS

The same problem of upper body and leg strength that exists in the shot also exists for the girls in the discus. You must encourage the girls to work with the weights as intensely as seems reasonable for each individual. Many girls will not have the balance and the leg strength necessary to execute the full, facing-the-rear three-quarter turn. If that is the case, do not hesitate to go back to the old side facing one-half turn. If they can't handle that, try a 1-2-3 walk across the circle just to gain a little momentum. Obviously, this sort of expedient is not appropriate for the girl with real potential in the event, but you are going to have to deal with a lot of girls for whom success in discus throwing is not going to be a major priority in life. For this type use whatever method across the circle gets the best results.

Although strength is a factor in the discus, it is not the strength event that the shot put is. Don't overlook the smaller, wiry girls, possibly from your running squad, as possible discus throwers. It is a beautiful and fluid event, one that suffers tremendously from attempting to muscle it out. The real keys are ability to master technique, relaxation, coordination, fluidity and patience. Look for young women who have these attributes, as well as for the larger types.

SAMPLE DISCUS WORK WEEK (MID-SEASON)

Monday:

30 min. Flexibility and warm-up
60 min. Heavy weight workout
15 min. 6 × 110's 80% walking in between
15 min. 3 × 220's 80% walking in between
15 min. Release drills
15 min. Standing throws

Tuesday:

30 min. Flexibility and warm-up
15 min. 10 × 10 yard races
15 min. Stair hopping drills
15 min. Standing throws
15 min. Circle work—discus taped to hand
30 min. Throwing through circle

Wednesday:

30 min. Flexibility and warm-up
15 min. Release drills
15 min. Standing throws
60 min. Explosive weight workout
15 min. 10 × downhill running
15 min. 10 × uphill running

Thursday:

30 min. Flexibility and warm-up
15 min. 2 × 40 yard dashes timed
15 min. 3 × Whistlers (Relaxation sprinting)
15 min. Standing throws
15 min. Circle work—discus taped to hand
30 min. Throwing through circle

Friday:

Rest or optional light loosening workout (Advanced)

Goal Day (Beginners)

Regular weight workout (Beginners)

Saturday:

Competition
Regular weight workout (Advanced)

CHAPTER 12

COACHING THE JAVELIN

A. PRESENTING THE EVENT

The javelin involves more aerodynamics and momentum than either of the other throwing events. In the classroom presentation to prospective javelin throwers, this point must be emphasized strongly. Of course, as in all throwing events, it is necessary to point out that the delivery angle and the velocity with which the implement leaves the hand are vital factors in determining distance, but the young athletes must be extremely aware that a stable flight of the javelin is absolutely essential if any kind of distance is to be achieved. Also, it should be emphasized that the javelin differs from the other throwing events in that there is no restriction on the amount of run-up that can be taken and, consequently, momentum becomes more of a factor than in events conducted within a confined area.

In spite of some rather significant differences in techniques utilized, the javelin, like the shot and discus, involves four basic stages: (1) momentum or run-up, (2) leading with the hip, (3) delivery, and (4) follow-through. In describing the momentum stage in this classroom presentation it should be pointed out that it really involves two phases, the initial run-up and a five-step sequence designed to continue acceleration and get the athlete into a proper throwing position. Leave the details of this to field instruction. You just want to get the basic idea across at this point.

In describing the next two stages, leading with the hip and delivery, the importance of whip action in throwing the javelin should be emphasized. We show pictures of the delivery action pointing out the "Bow" or "C" position of the body and emphasizing the absolutely essential factor of keeping the javelin straight. In discussing the follow-through we utilize the same basic description of this phase of throwing events that we employed with the shot put and is described in that chapter. In fact, it can be a timesaving procedure if all throwing event prospects can be brought together for that presentation. Again, the importance of throwing off the front leg and bringing the rear leg through after and not before the release is an essential understanding to establish at this point. As in all field events, the showing of loop films to give the athlete a feel for the event is an extremely important phase of the initial classroom session.

B. TEACHING THE JAVELIN

1. The grip and carry

The teaching process for the javelin should begin with the grip and carry position. We tell our athletes to place the binding in the V of the palm of the hand with the second finger gripping the binding edge. We discourage the use of the first finger grip because it is not as efficient. It is more natural, however, and youngsters will move to it if you are not careful. The "Fork" grip is a widely used technique and may well be superior for some individuals. There is absolutely no quarrel here with starting beginners with this grip if that is a coach's preference. It is important to start all beginners off with the same basic grip to avoid confusion. At some point along the line, however, a promising thrower should be introduced to the alternate grip. It may be that either the "Fork" or "Second Finger" may be the most effective grip for a particular individual. You would make a serious mistake not to make that determination, but do not confuse the youngster by giving this choice while still in the learning process.

We teach a carry over the right shoulder, about three to four inches above the head, in a relaxed position. We teach the athletes to carry the point slightly down as this aids in keeping the javelin in line during the withdrawal. Many javelin throwers do not carry with the point down, and I do not argue this point, but youngsters at this level seem to control the javelin better in the withdrawal if they have a better vision of the point.

2. The five-step transition phase

Teaching the transition step at this point is a bit of a contradiction when compared to the methods of teaching the shot put and discus advocated in this book. The momentum factor and the complexity of getting into a throwing position from the run-up lend themselves, in my judgment, to teaching the javelin throwing position as part of a five-step sequence rather than simply as a standing throw.

We use the Finnish style with a five-step sequence. As has been said previously, this book is not a technique manual, and we assume the reader's knowledge of basic technique. There is nothing sacred about a five-step transition approach, but it is my experience that beginners are most comfortable with this technique. In learning the five-step sequence, the athlete completes the run-up on the right foot (right-handed thrower) and begins the transition steps with the left foot.

In teaching this process, walk the youngsters through the five steps by the numbers, constantly checking to be sure they are executing properly. The first two steps involve the withdrawal of the javelin and should not be considered a crossover. Emphasize running by the javelin, not jerking it backward. The key coaching point here is to be sure the athlete keeps the javelin straight. The withdrawal should be complete by the time the right foot strikes the ground on the second step and should be completed with the throwing hand, palm up, at shoulder level with the javelin as close to the body as possible, straight and positioned at an angle running through the hair line, just above the forehead. The left arm is curled across the chest and the throwing arm is straight, but the elbow must not be locked. (See Figure 12.1.)

The key on steps 3 and 4 is to get into the throwing position. This is where the crossover takes place. The coaching points to emphasize here are to point the feet 23 degrees to the right (right-handed throwers), turn the shoulders 90 degrees to the line of flight while keeping the hips as much to the front as possible, and gaining a backward lean. (See Figure 12.2.)

The fifth step begins before the fourth lands and a sort of bounding action results. The rhythm you are looking for is not 1 - 2 - 3 - 45, but rather 1 - 2 - 3 - 45. When teaching this as a walk-through, this point is not important, but the athlete should be made aware of it and as soon as you start to put the process into a run it should be introduced.

The key coaching points on the fifth step are as follows: (1) the left leg lands heel first with the toe pointing in the direction of the line of flight. The left leg lands straight but will begin to bend as soon as it makes contact; (2) the right knee and foot should be turned inward and pointing in the direction of line of flight; (3) as soon as the left heel strikes the ground, drive the right leg and hip vigorously forward, with the head tilted up and slightly to the left with the back arched so that the body forms the classic, and very distinct, "Bow" position. (See Figure 12.3.)

FIGURE 12.1
Position-Transition Step 2

FIGURE 12.2
Position-Transition Step 4

FIGURE 12.3
"Bow" or "C" Position

3. The delivery

It is obviously better for the athlete if you can teach the delivery individually, but if you have numerous javelin candidates it is not very practical. We save every broken javelin we have and use them with our beginners. At this stage, the teaching of the delivery action is important, the flight of the javelin is of no interest. We line all the youngsters across the field in a straight line, all facing in the same direction, each with his or her own javelin, and all go through the process together.

(1) The first step is to walk through the five steps and stop as the left heel makes contact with the ground. On the coach's command "Rock" they drive the rear foot and hip forward, rocking the left or front foot from the heel onto the ball of the foot with the body assuming the "Bow" position and the javelin still back. On the command "Pull" they all deliver the javelin over the left leg with no follow-through. The key coaching points here are as follows. 1. Lead the elbow, keeping it up and out with the right or throwing hand above the elbow and well to its inside. This is absolutely essential to keep the javelin straight and to protect the elbow from undue strain, resulting in what is often called tennis elbow. 2. Pull the javelin through in one smooth motion. 3. Throw through the point, releasing well ahead of the body at the maximum point of upward pull. 4. Release with an outward snap of the wrist.

(2) The second step is exactly the same as the first except that when the coach gives the command "Rock," the athletes execute the Rock and Pull in sequence but all at once in a smooth motion.

(3) The third step involves walking through the first two steps of the transition approach, with the coach checking to be sure the javelin has been properly withdrawn. Then on the coach's command "Go," the athletes execute the final three steps culminating in the Rock and Pull.

(4) The fourth step involves putting the entire five-step approach together. As soon as the athlete can do this reasonably well, we introduce the follow-through. This is done much earlier in the teaching process than in the shot and discus. The reason for this is that momentum is so vital in the javelin that you may have difficulty gaining it if you have the youngsters throw too long without a follow-through. It is essential to teach the delivery at first without a follow-through, however, to be sure the athlete is throwing off the front leg. In the javelin, however, you must teach throwing up and over the front leg and that is going to be hard to do without a follow-through. Consequently, introduce the follow-through fairly early in the teaching process, but continually emphasize that the rear leg does not come through until the javelin leaves the hand. (See Figure 12.4.)

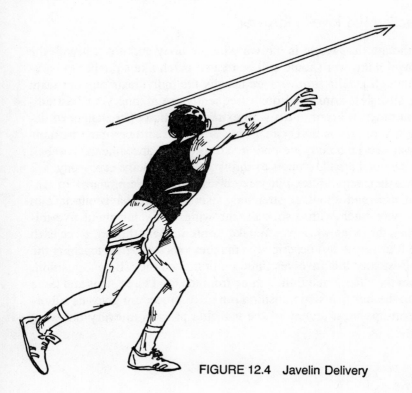

FIGURE 12.4   Javelin Delivery

5. *Drill for backward lean and the crossover:* To teach youngsters to get the rhythm and bounding action of the fourth and fifth steps of the transition approach and to emphasize backward lean on steps 3 - 4 - 5, have them run the length of the field doing one crossover after another with a good backward lean. Do it at first without a javelin and then add the javelin to the drill.

4. Adding momentum or the run-up

Once a reasonable technique is established from the five-step-approach, then begin to add the run-up phase. Start off by teaching a four-step run just to get a little momentum and the feel of combining the five-step transition with a run-up. Once they get the hang of this, go up to an eight-step run. We like to have our javelin throwers use an eight-step run up when they begin competing and eventually move up to a twelve-step run if they can handle it. Emphasize a very slow run-up at first, constantly emphasizing that a key to successful javelin throwing is acceleration, and the five-step transition actually involves a picking up of speed from the run-up.

C. TRAINING THE HIGH SCHOOL JAVELIN THROWER

1. Protecting the javelin thrower

Although the javelin is thrown with the body and not just with the arm, a javelin thrower should still be treated much like a pitcher in base-ball. Although javelin throwers are usually the individuals on your team with the strongest arms, and quite frequently are among your best ath-letes, you must still train them with extreme caution. The danger of de-veloping a sore arm is a very real one. A javelin thrower must be thor-oughly warmed-up before attempting to throw hard, and, like the baseball pitcher, cannot be called upon to throw at full capacity every day.

After their regular flexibility exercises with the team, warm-up run-ning and arm and shoulder stretching exercises, we have our javelin throwers play catch with a softball, throwing easily for about five mi-nutes. In all throwing workouts we take 12 preliminary throws, three each from the four stages just described in the previous section on teaching the javelin. Basically this involves three pulling from the "Bow" position, three from the "Rock and Pull," three from the final three steps and three more with the full five-step transition run. This procedure gives us a thor-ough warm-up and a review of the teaching process in every throwing workout.

We never allow our javelin competitors to throw all-out two days in a row. Hard throwing on cold, wet days, a not unusual phenomenon in New England, especially in the early spring, should be avoided as much as possible. It is also very important to check with every javelin thrower each day on the condition of his or her arm. If an athlete complains of soreness, do not force that individual to throw. Of course, being this cautious involves the risk of babying your athletes. Some will take advantage of the situation and conveniently develop a sore arm whenever they do not feel like working hard. In my judgment, this is a risk you have to take. It is better to be over-cautious than to ruin a good prospect's arm. Don't worry about the fakers who may get out of a little work. That type is never going to help you in the long run anyway.

In training javelin throwers, be especially careful in dealing with the individuals who have particularly poor technique. A youngster who fails to lead with the elbow when delivering is going to be extremely susceptible to arm soreness and tennis elbow. Technique in javelin throwing is not just a means of gaining greater distances, it is a major factor in protecting the young athlete. It is usually unwise to send an athlete off alone to work on an event, but, if you are ever tempted to do so, the javelin is one event where the temptation must be resisted.

2. Technique training

Since our javelin coach also handles the discus and shot, the best we can hope for is supervision of javelin technique training one-third of the time in our normal practice sessions. It is possible to get a decent amount of throwing in a relatively short time, even with large numbers of throwers, if you line them up in a straight line across the field under the coach's direct supervision and throw more than one athlete at a time. On a field of 60 yards width, we have thrown 10 athletes at once, working the "Pull" from the "Bow" position and the "Rock and Pull" drills previously described. We have spread five athletes across the same field utilizing the final three- and five-step throwing drills, and have thrown three at a time utilizing the full run-up. Of course, the ability of the coach to analyze and correct faults diminishes in direct proportion to the number of youngsters throwing at any one time. It boils down to a matter of priorities. If you have large numbers of throwers and a limited amount of direct supervision time, using the above system makes sense. It is also effective in going through the previously described four stages of preliminary warm-up throws in a short period of time. If you use this procedure it's vitally important to make sure everyone throws at the same time and only upon command. It is also vital that everyone goes out into the field to retrieve the javelins at the same time and only upon the coach's command.

i. The run-up and approach

A javelin thrower must be trained in executing a uniform run the same way all jumpers and pole vaulters must. Running the same number of steps in exactly the same way every time is just as important for the javelin thrower as for any jumper. This includes developing uniformity in the five-step transition approach just as much as it does for the run-up. This process must become as uniform as possible as it has to become automatic when executing the actual throw. If an athlete is thinking steps and worrying about fouling, he or she is simply not going to achieve anywhere near maximum performance.

Whether you use one or two check marks is a matter of personal preference. I like to start off javelin throwers with just a starting point mark. If it appears an individual is having difficulty with steps or might increase confidence if a second check is included, then add one. Don't put the second check too close to the toe board, however, so that the youngster cannot pull up and abort the throw if he or she misses it. If an athlete misses a check mark and still has to go through with the throw, all you have succeeded in accomplishing with the second check mark is destroying the youngster's concentration and confidence.

In determining the starting point for the run-up, have each athlete work with two partners and do not use a toe board. One partner counts the run-up steps and the five transition steps to be sure the individual throwing has executed whatever number of steps (usually eight and five) have been determined for that particular individual. The second partner marks where the athlete ended up after completing the throw and follow-through. When this finishing point begins to get consistent, measure the distance back from the finish point to the starting point, add a foot as a safety factor, and this distance becomes the measurement from the toe board to the initial starting mark. Having a partner count the steps is absolutely essential as javelin throwers are very prone to mixing up the proper number of steps on the run-up. Where they end up is meaningless if they do not take the prescribed number of steps.

ii. Utilizing partners in working on technique

As in the shot and discus, we also utilize partners in assisting the coach to analyze an athlete's throw. In the javelin I like to employ four partner assistants. The first counts steps to be sure the athlete has not fouled up the run-up. A second marks the spot where the delivery and follow-through were concluded. The third partner stands behind the thrower and checks to be sure the javelin has remained straight throughout the execution, while the fourth looks for the position of the throwing hand at the start of the pull to assist in checking for delivery angle. Obviously, there is nothing sacred about four partners. You can have as many youngsters as you wish checking on whatever areas you wish. The system is effective because it enhances your ability as the coach to analyze each throw and it keeps the athletes involved and constantly learning. As has been said over and over in this book, the coach should zero in on just one aspect of each throw as you cannot effectively watch more than one thing at a time.

3. Strength training

We use the same basic strength training program for javelin throwers as we do for those in the shot and discus. The only difference is that we cut down a little more for javelin throwers as soon as the competitive season begins. Once the competition begins we eliminate the heavy lift workouts and we lift regular-explosive two days a week. We absolutely never lift the day before competition or an attempt to throw for distance, and we avoid lifting two days before major competition. We encourage all our javelin throwers to work on throwing two-to-four pound iron balls every other day, alternating with weight training, in the off season. Also in our strength program is a partner-type exercise in which the full pull of the javelin delivery is executed with the partner applying resistance. We

Free Weight Program	Weight Machine Program
Bench press	Bench press
Military press	Military press
Lateral raise	Front trunk twists
Squats	Forearm curls
Heel raises	Upright rowing
Clean and jerk	Lateral raise
Forearm curls	Kneeling pulldowns
Upright rowing	Dips
Inclined sit-ups	Leg press
Leg lifts	Inclined sit-ups
Leg extensions	Leg lifts
Leg curls	Leg extensions
	Leg curls

have them do three sets of ten repetitions of this exercise, making sure all repetitions are executed in good form and the resistance is of such a nature that an eleventh repetition could not be executed in good form. The same exercise can be accomplished with an old javelin handle attached to a wall-type pulley exerciser.

4. Running workouts

Essentially the javelin thrower is given the same 30 minutes a day of running workouts that we give the shot-putters and discus throwers. The javelin throwers' program includes the same type of downhill running, uphill running, 40 yard dashes and Whistlers we give our sprinters. Since the run-up is such an integral part of javelin throwing, it is important to give the javelin throwers a lot of form and uniform running work. It is not a bad idea to include your javelin throwers with the long jumpers and triple jumpers when they are working on uniform running.

D. ANALYZING THE MOST COMMON FAULTS IN HIGH SCHOOL JAVELIN THROWERS

1. Failure to maintain acceleration

i Cause

Failure to maintain acceleration is inevitably caused by starting off too fast in the run-up.

ii. Correction

The correction is simple—start off slowly. The youngsters must be made to realize it is acceleration in the last five steps that counts, not how fast they run with the javelin. It is far better to start off very slowly in the run-up so that acceleration is possible in the transition steps, than it is to build up a tremendous amount of momentum and then lose it as the throw commences. Most high school javelin throwers are decelerating rather than accelerating when they execute the throw. The key to acceleration is a slow, gradual build-up in the run. If an athlete starts off too fast, it is virtually impossible to transfer into the proper throwing technique in the final three steps. Constantly emphasize acceleration and utilize the repeated crossover drill previously described to impress upon the youngsters that the transition phase does not necessitate a slowing down. Too fast an early run is almost certainly going to result in a drastic slowing down or in loss of control, either of which is going to cause serious problems.

2. Failure to keep the javelin straight

i. Cause

This problem is caused mainly either by an improper withdrawal letting the javelin get away from the body, or by the failure to lead with the elbow during delivery.

ii. Correction

In teaching the withdrawal, emphasize running by the javelin keeping it close to the body, instead of jerking it out and to the rear. There is a definite tendency for beginners to jerk the javelin back. If a youngster is having extreme trouble in the withdrawal, try going to a seven-step transition allowing four strides to withdraw the javelin. This shouldn't be necessary, but some individuals just cannot seem to withdraw smoothly in two steps. It will never take anyone four steps to execute a withdrawal, but allowing them to start the mental process sooner can help certain individuals.

If the elbow is not leading properly, emphasize bringing the wrist up over the ear and keeping it inside the elbow. If the wrist is over or outside of the elbow as the javelin is pulled through, the thrower is not only going to get a curve ball and consequent severe loss of distance, but is also a prime candidate for a very sore arm and tennis elbow.

3. Failure to achieve the "Bow" position

i. Cause

Failure to achieve the "Bow" position is almost always the result of being over-anxious and trying to execute the throw too soon. Without the "Bow" position the athlete has failed to lead with the hip and has lost the whip action so essential to good javelin throwing.

ii. Correction

Achieving the "Bow" position is the result of developing proper habits in the learning process. Teaching the javelin delivery in the four stages described previously and requiring the athletes to start off each technique workout with 12 throws, three each from the stages described will help tremendously in getting the athlete into the proper throwing position. Losing control is also a major factor here and slowing down the approach run will enhance the chances of getting into the proper "Bow" position.

4. Improper angle of incidence of the javelin in flight

In simpler terms this means either tail drag while in flight or the javelin's taking a nose dive, almost like a drop thrown by a baseball pitcher.

i. Cause

Tail drag is the result of releasing the javelin too soon and is usually caused once again by over-anxiousness. The athlete must release at the maximum extension of the upward movement or pull. If the javelin is released before that point it will usually go off to the right with a considerable tail drag and consequent stalling. If the javelin takes a nose dive, it is the result of holding on too long. Instead of releasing at the top of the pull, the athlete has released with a downward snap of the wrist. To avoid the nose dive, be sure the release takes place at the top of the pull, before the downward action of the wrist.

ii. Correction

Constantly emphasize throwing through the point. Some of our javelin throwers have been helped by getting them to think of the delivery as a pull-push-pull action. The delivery is started with a pull and as the javelin passes the shoulder it actually develops into a pushing action. The release comes at the end of the push and before the pulling begins again, a process which is actually the follow-through.

Another factor to look for here is a premature bending or cocking of the arm before the pull begins. This is a natural tendency, but results in loss of leverage and makes it extremely difficult to execute throwing through the point.

5. Improper delivery angle

i. Cause

A major cause of an improper delivery angle is the placement of the throwing hand upon withdrawal of the javelin. It is a common tendency to drop the hand much too low. A second factor is that many young throwers intentionally try to get too much height under the mistaken impression that added height will make the implement go farther.

ii. Correction

Experts now estimate the ideal angle of delivery in the javelin to be lower than that in the shot and discus, roughly around 30–35 degrees. It is essential to see to it that the athlete fully understands proper delivery angle. If a youngster is getting too much height without intentionally seeking it, then it is likely the result of dropping the throwing hand below the shoulder level in the withdrawal. Frequently, you will see some throwers actually hitting the ground with the tail of the javelin just before the delivery.

Too high a delivery angle will often result in stalling, as will too high an angle of incidence or tail dragging, particularly if throwing against the wind. The great throwers get best distance throwing into the wind as the same principle applies as when an airplane takes off into the wind. This is true, but only with proper angle of delivery and angle of incidence. Throwing too high and/or achieving tail drag into the wind will result in an absolute disaster.

6. Improper follow through

i. Cause

Some javelin thrower, like their shot and discus counterparts, will bring everything at once, hip, right arm and right leg. At least as common with javelin throwers is the opposite extreme, failing to take full advantage of the follow-through. If a thrower is properly getting up over the front leg in the delivery, and taking full advantage of the run-up and acceleration, a good follow-through is an absolute necessity.

ii. Correction

If everything is coming at once and the follow-through is taking place before the delivery is complete, slow the youngster down and get him or her under control. As in all throwing events, this fault is going to take place if you cannot curb over-anxiousness and the natural desire to throw too soon. If it is the other extreme that is the problem, the chances are the athlete is too conscious of the toe board. Work on the run-up and marks to eliminate concern about fouling. There is no way an individual can throw aggressively if he is worried about steps and fouling. Set the check marks so that the throw is made with plenty of room to spare from the toe board. Most good javelin throwers will bounce two or three times off the right foot after making the reverse. It is far better to give oneself an extra three to four feet back from the toe board and utilize the extra distance to recover from the throw, getting full momentum in the process, than it is to get real close to the toe board with a resulting holding back to avoid fouling. A few feet lost in back of the toe board in order to get everything into a throw, is more than offset by the added distance gained on the other end.

E. SPECIAL PROBLEMS IN COACHING
GIRL JAVELIN THROWERS

Since strength is not as much of a factor in javelin throwing as it is in the shot and discus, there really is little need to consider teaching and training girls any differently from the boys. Since many girls may not have the athletic background of the boys, and may not have done as much throwing of baseballs, footballs, etc., it may be necessary to handle a girl's arm with even more caution than her male counterpart. The average girl can probably not handle as much hard throwing as the average boy. The more you know about a girl's athletic background, the more intelligently you can determine how much hard throwing you can give her.

In discussing the shot an discus throws for girls, the possibility was expressed that a simpler style for some girls may be appropriate. This is an expediency that should never be employed with any individual who has definite potential for success in an event. In the case of a girl who is obviously never going to throw the javelin again after high school, and cannot master whatever style you are teaching, it might be appropriate to teach the old American hop or the simple three-step background crossover. If it means more success for the girl and points for your team, don't hesitate to employ a simpler and more effective style.

F. SELECTION OF THE JAVELIN

The final point to be made in regard to the javelin is the selection for each individual of the implement itself. The superiority of the aerodynamic javelin has been well established. We don't however, let any of our beginners use the aerodynamic javelin until they have demonstrated they can throw at least 140-150 feet for the boys and 90-100 feet for the girls with a regular implement. We do this to protect the more expensive javelins, but also because we feel the aerodynamic javelin is more likely to stall and has far more disadvantages than advantages for the weak thrower. All decent throwers, however, should use the aerodynamic javelin.

We have always understood that aerodynamic javelins are calibrated for certain ideal distances; the 55-meter javelin is designed for throwers in roughly the 175-foot category, the 60-meter for 191-foot throwers and the 70-meter for those who can throw around 220 feet. An athlete using a javelin calibrated for distances beyond what the individual can throw will result in stalling and lesser distance. Statements made by experts at clinics I have attended and my own recent experience indicate this factor may not be true for all individuals. Athletes are using 70- and 80-meter javelins and are winning with throws in the 190-220 foot range with javelins calibrated for much greater distances. Don't be scared off by the 70- or 80-meter javelins, or any aerodynamic javelin for that matter. Let each javelin thrower experiment and come up with the javelin that gives him or her the best results. Athletes who tend to throw too high or to develop tail drag will probably have the least success with javelins calibrated beyond their throwing range, especially if they are throwing into the wind. Experiment, nevertheless, with all your throwers. You could well be losing in this event simply because a youngster is not using the type of javelin best suited for his particular needs.

SAMPLE JAVELIN WORK WEEK (MID-SEASON)

Monday:

30 min. Flexibility and warm-up
15 min. 6 × 110's 80% walking in between
15 min. Play catch warm-up
30 min. Pull, rock, 3-step, 5-step drills
30 min. Full run throws
15 min. 3 × 220's 80% walking in between

Tuesday:

30 min. Flexibility and warm-up
15 min. Uniform running work
15 min. 10 × 10 yard races
15 min. Crossover running drills with javelin
15 min. Work on steps and full run
60 min. Regular weight workout

Wednesday:

30 min. Flexibility and warm-up
15 min. 10 × downhill running
15 min. Play catch warm-up
30 min. Pull, rock, 3-step, 5-step drills
30 min. Full run throws
15 min. 10 × uphill running

Thursday:

15 min. 2 × 40 yard dashes timed
15 min. 3 × Whistlers (Relaxation sprinting)
15 min. Crossover running drills with javelin
15 min. Work on steps and full run
60 min. Explosive weight workout

Friday:

Rest or optional light loosening workout (Advanced)

Goal Day (Beginners)

Saturday:

Competition

Index